LET'S EAT

Thai

HERE'S A quick way to make tasty and filling minestrone soup.

Bring about 1½ pints of salted water to the boil and add ½ cup broken spaghetti or crushed macaroni. Cook for 5 minutes, then add 8 oz packet frozen mixed vegetables and bring back to the boil for a further 5 minutes.

Recipe

Meanwhile, cook 4 rashers of chopped bacon gently until the fat runs, then add chopped onion or leek and fry for 7 to 8 minutes without browning.

Drain pasta and vegetables and return to pan. Add 1 pint stock, large can of tomato soup and drained bacon and onion. Reheat and season. Serve with grated hard cheese and chopped parsley.

Plan and

FOR THE next two weeks we'll look at some travel news and pick the best of the winter and summer '93 bargains.

Thomas Cook, Thomsons and the Owners Abroad group have already launched their 1993 brochures. Incentives to book early include discounts of up to £150 per person on a £1 deposit from Thomas Cook.

Thomsons offer excellent deals for families, plus lots of early booking offers. For example, £100 off all child prices to Florida.

They've also trebled the number of free kids places on Skytours, with child prices starting from £74 for 14 nights, Glasgow-Majorca.

Falcon, like the others, is also offering aggressive price cuts for next summer, competition which should benefit the consumer.

LET'S EAT Thai

Supenn Vudinantha

Editor
Wendy Hobson

foulsham
LONDON • NEW YORK • TORONTO • SYDNEY

foulsham

Yeovil Road, Slough, Berkshire, SL1 4JH

ISBN 0-572-01799-5

Photoset in Great Britain by Encounter Photosetting, Fleet, Hampshire
Printed in Great Britain by Cox & Wyman Ltd, Reading, Berkshire

Contents

1. **Introduction**   6
   Ingredients
   Equipment
   Cooking Methods
   Notes on the Recipes

2. **Appetisers**   17
3. **Soups**   31
4. **Seafood**   41
5. **Poultry**   59
6. **Meat**   74
7. **Vegetable Dishes**   87
8. **Noodles and Rice**   96
9. **Salads**   109
10. **Desserts and Breads**   124
11. **Drinks**   137
12. **Sauces**   142
    Index   156

Introduction

Thai food is a wonderful and unique culinary experience. Although it has been influenced in the past by the cooking styles of its neighbours – noticeably China and India – it always finds new and unmistakeably Thai ways of adopting and adapting ingredients and recipes. It has made the Chinese-style technique of stir-frying its own with many lightly cooked dishes, while the mellow-flavoured Thai curries, often made with coconut milk, are reminiscent of many Indian dishes.

One of the key features of Thai cooking – as in all the best cuisine – is their use of the freshest and best quality ingredients available. The street markets in Thai towns and villages abound with a vast range of fresh fruits, vegetables, herbs and spices which are carefully selected to create the finest dishes. Some may be exotic to Western taste, but we have only included ingredients in the recipes in this book which are readily available in supermarkets or occasionally in delicatessens or oriental food shops.

Herbs and spices, too, are very important in Thai cooking.
Ginger and garlic, basil and coriander, black pepper and lemon juice feature heavily in many of the dishes. Since fresh herbs are now the first things on display in most large supermarkets, it is no problem to find delicious fresh herbs with which to flavour your cooking.

As with many countries, different styles of cooking prevail in different areas. In the south, there are many seafood dishes and curries and chillis feature high on the list of ingredients.

Central Thailand is sometimes known as the 'rice bowl', so not surprisingly there are many rice dishes served with spicy sauces.

Further north, grilled meats are served with rich spicy sauces and accompanied by short-grain rice dishes rather than the long-grain rice more popular elsewhere.

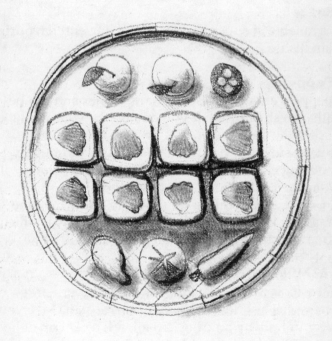

Ingredients

All the ingredients used in the recipes are readily available
in the West, most of them in large supermarkets and just a
few from delicatessens or oriental food shops.

Bamboo Shoots
These are available canned and should be drained before use.

Bean Sauce
This is available in supermarkets and is a useful flavouring
for Asian dishes.

Chilli Peppers
Chilli peppers are used to spice many dishes and can be
used either fresh or dried. If you do not like your food too
hot, discard the seeds when you prepare them. In any
event, make sure that you wash your hands thoroughly
after touching chillis as they contain an irritant which will
sting your eyes or mouth if you touch them.

If you do not have chillis, you can substitute cayenne
pepper, which is made from hot chillis, or paprika, which is
made from milder chillis. You can also use chilli paste.

Coconut Milk and Cream
Coconut milk is available canned in some supermarkets or
in delicatessens or oriental food shops. You can make your
own coconut milk by pouring 250 ml/8 fl oz/1 cup of hot
water over 100 g/4 oz shredded coconut and leaving over a
low heat for about 30 minutes. Strain the milk into a bowl
through a piece of muslin and squeeze out as much liquid
as possible.

Coconut cream is also available canned and is much
thicker; more like the texture of double cream. Blocks of
creamed coconut are not the same. These can be used for
grating.

Fish Sauce

Thai fish sauce, or *nam pla*, is a thin, salty brown sauce
which is widely used in Thai cooking instead of salt. It is
made by pressing salted fish and is available in oriental
food shops. You should adjust the amount you use
according to your personal taste.

Ginger

Root ginger is often used in Thai cooking. It should be
peeled before use and then chopped, sliced or grated,
according to the recipe. You can buy it in small pieces so
that it is always fresh.

Herbs and Spices

Favourite herbs in Thai cooking are bay leaves, coriander,
mint and basil, all of which are available in supermarkets or
you can grow your own in the garden, if you have one, so
that you always have fresh herbs available.

Cardamom, cayenne pepper, cumin, cinnamon and
cloves are all used in Thai cooking. Garam masala and five-
spice powder are also popular.

Lemon Grass

A gently lemon-flavoured herb which is very popular in
cooking, this is available fresh or dried in specialist shops.
Dried lemon grass needs to be soaked before use. If you do
not have it, substitute a little grated lemon rind, but not too
much as this will have a sharper taste.

Limes

It is better to use fresh lime and lime juice in the recipes,
and these are now readily available in most large
supermarkets.

Dried Mushrooms

Chinese dried mushrooms are available in delicatessens or
oriental food shops. They need to be soaked for about 30
minutes in hot water then drained well. Discard the hard

stems and use the caps as directed in the recipe.

Noodles

Thai recipes use both transparent or cellophane noodles, the slightly thicker rice noodles, flat rice noodles and also egg noodles. These are available in supermarkets or delicatessens.

Oyster Sauce

Oriental oyster sauce is often used as a flavouring in Thai cooking. It is widely available in supermarkets.

Prawns and Shellfish

If you use cooked prawns in the recipes, only cook them for the minimum amount of time or they will go rubbery. If you can, find uncooked prawns as these will give the best flavour. Cook them for about 4 to 5 minutes, just until they turn pink.

Clams and mussels should be soaked in several changes of fresh water so that the clams or mussels can filter out any grit. They should then be scrubbed, the beards cut off the mussels and be well rinsed. Any clams which remain open when tapped should be discarded and also any clams which do not open when cooked.

Rice

Some Thai dishes use sticky shorter-grained rice, and it is best to look for Italian, Arborio or medium-grain rice for these dishes in order to get an authentic result. Other dishes use the long-grain rice which is more popular in the West, and you can use basmati or any other long-grain rice you prefer.

Shallots

Shallots are often used in Thai cooking as they have a more delicate flavour than onions. If you do not have them, you can substitute onions or spring onions.

Shrimp Paste
Thai shrimp paste is a dark brown, dry paste used to flavour sauces. It is available in oriental food stores. If it is not available, it can be omitted from the recipes in this book.

Tamarind
In the UK, tamarind is generally available as a concentrated paste made from tamarind pulp. It is used in small quantities to give a sweet and sour flavour to dishes.

Water Chestnuts
These are readily available canned and should be drained well before use.

Won Ton Wrappers
These are available in oriental food stores and are used for wrapping tiny pastries or egg rolls. You can use filo pastry instead if you cannot find them.

Yellow Bean Paste
This is sometimes used to flavour Thai dishes and is available in supermarkets and oriental food stores.

Equipment

There is no real need for special equipment for cooking the recipes in this book, just use your normal kitchen equipment. A few special items may be useful, but you can always substitute something else.

Clay Pots
Traditional unglazed clay pots were used for Thai curries, soups and rice dishes. They have now largely been replaced by modern metal or porcelain dishes, although if you do use one, remember to soak it in water for at least an hour before use and never place a hot unglazed pottery utensil on a cool surface.

Mortar and Pestle
These are traditionally used to crush spices, herbs or other ingredients.

Steamer
A steamer with a tight-fitting lid is useful for some dishes so that the food can be cooked gently above boiling water. Chinese bamboo steamers are ideal. Place the food on a heatproof plate inside the steamer and cover with another plate. If you do not have one, you can use a metal colander or heatproof bowl placed over a saucepan.

Wok
A wok is the best utensil for stir-frying as its shape means that it needs little oil, the food is cooked quickly, and it can be stirred easily without spilling over the edges. If you do not have a wok, a large frying pan can be used instead.

Cooking Methods

These recipes have been prepared so that they are simple for the Western cook to follow. The cooking methods are familiar to all cooks: stir-frying; frying; steaming; braising; roasting.

Skinning Tomatoes
To skin a tomato, cut a cross on the top and immerse it in boiling water for about 1 minute. Lift it out of the water with a slotted spoon and place in cold water until cool enough to handle. The skin should slip off fairly easily. You can deseed tomatoes before chopping, if you prefer.

Preparing Chilli Peppers
These can be used whole, sliced or chopped in different recipes. Remove the stem and inner membranes and discard the seeds unless you like a particularly hot dish. You can always add a few seeds once you have experimented with some of the dishes.

Always remember to wash your hands after you have prepared chilli peppers as they contain an irritant which will sting your mouth or eyes if you touch them.

Notes on the Recipes

1. Follow one set of measurements only, do not mix metric and Imperial.

2. Eggs are size 2.

3. Wash fresh produce before preparation.

4. Spoon measurements are level.

5. Adjust seasoning and strongly-flavoured ingredients, such as onions and garlic, to suit your own taste.

6. If you substitute dried for fresh herbs, use only half the amount specified.

Appetisers

Like the Chinese, the Thais often serve a selection of appetisers to start a meal, each guest trying a little of the range of delicacies on offer.

1 Deep-Fried Fish Cakes

Ingredients

225 g/8 oz cod fillet, minced
1 onion, finely chopped
1 stick lemon grass, finely chopped
15 ml/1 tbsp chopped fresh parsley
1 chilli pepper, chopped
15 ml/1 tbsp fish sauce
1 egg
30 ml/2 tbsp cornflour
Pinch of sugar
Oil for deep-frying

Method

1. Blend all the ingredients together well and shape into small fish cakes.

2. Heat the oil and fry the fish cakes for about 10 minutes until golden brown. Drain on kitchen paper and serve hot with Cucumber Sauce (page 146).

Serves 4

2 Crispy-Fried Noodles

Ingredients

150 ml/ 1/4 pt/ 2/3 cup water
75 g/3 oz/ 1/3 cup soft brown sugar
30 ml/2 tbsp fish sauce
15 ml/1 tbsp red wine vinegar
5 ml/1 tsp tamarind pulp
5 ml/1 tsp tomato ketchup
Oil for deep-frying
100 g/4 oz rice noodles
100 g/4 oz cooked chicken, diced
50 g/2 oz cooked peeled prawns, chopped
50 g/2 oz beansprouts
2 spring onions, chopped
2 red chilli peppers, sliced
2 sprigs fresh coriander

Method

1. Mix together the water, sugar, fish sauce, wine vinegar, tamarind pulp and tomato ketchup. Bring to the boil then cover and simmer for 40 minutes until slightly thickened.

2. Heat the oil and fry the noodles a few at a time until puffed up. Drain well on kitchen paper.

3. Mix the noodles carefully with the chicken, prawns, beansprouts and onions. Toss gently with the sauce, garnish with the chilli peppers and parsley and serve immediately.

Serves 4

3 Coconut Squid Kebabs

Ingredients

450 g/1 lb squid
10 ml/2 tsp grated ginger root
400 ml/14 fl oz/1 ³/₄ cups coconut cream
5 ml/1 tsp turmeric
5 ml/1 tsp fish sauce
A pinch of curry powder
10 ml/2 tsp vegetable oil
1 clove garlic, crushed

Method

1.   To prepare the squid, pull the tentacles away from the body and remove the skin. Cut off and discard the plastic-like quill, the eyes and beak. Cut the body into pieces.

2.   Bring a large saucepan of water to the boil and blanch the squid briefly, in batches if necessary, until it turns opaque. Remove and drain.

3.   Mix together the ginger, 250 ml/8 fl oz/1 cup of coconut cream, the turmeric, fish sauce and curry powder. Add the squid and coat well. Thread the squid pieces on to skewers, arrange in a baking tin and pour over the remaining marinade. Leave to stand for 2 hours.

4.   Meanwhile, heat the oil and fry the garlic until just beginning to brown. Remove from the heat and blend in the remaining coconut cream.

5.   Preheat the grill. Baste the squid kebabs generously with the garlic cream and grill for a few

minutes, turning once or twice and basting with the cream as they cook. Serve at once.

Serves 4

4 | Grilled Scallops

Ingredients

30 ml/2 tbsp butter or margarine
2 spring onions, chopped
225 g/8 oz button mushrooms
Freshly ground black pepper
120 ml/4 fl oz/1/2 cup coconut milk
450 g/1 lb shelled scallops
10 ml/2 tsp vegetable oil
1 clove garlic, crushed
175 ml/6 fl oz/3/4 cup coconut cream

Method

1.   Melt the butter or margarine and fry the onions
      and mushrooms for about 5 minutes until lightly
      browned. Season with pepper.

2.   Remove from the heat and stir in the coconut milk.
      Add the scallops and leave to stand for 2 hours.

3.   Meanwhile, heat the oil and fry the garlic until just
      browned. Remove from the heat and blend in the
      coconut cream.

4.   Arrange the scallops and mushrooms alternately
      on skewers in a baking tin and pour over the
      remaining marinade. Chill.

5.   Preheat the grill. Baste the kebabs with the garlic
      cream and grill for about 4 minutes each side,
      basting with the garlic cream.

Serves 4

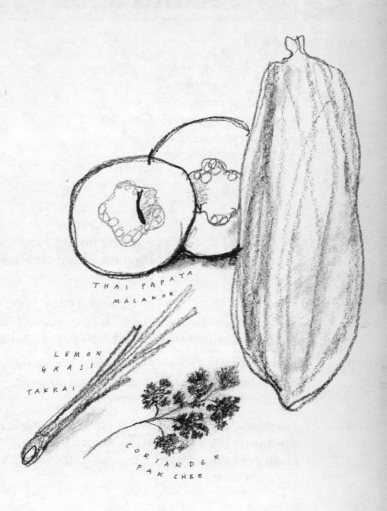

THAI PAPAYA
MALAKOR

LEMON
GRASS

TAKRAI

CORIANDER
PAK CHEE

5   Sweet and Sour Eggs

Ingredients

15 ml/1 tbsp vegetable oil
3 spring onions, sliced
Oil for deep-frying
4 hard-boiled eggs, peeled and halved
30 ml/2 tbsp soft brown sugar
30 ml/2 tbsp fish sauce
1 red chilli pepper, chopped
2 sprigs coriander

Method

1.   Heat the oil and fry the spring onions for a few minutes until lightly browned. Drain on kitchen paper.

2.   Heat the oil for deep-frying and fry the eggs, flat side down, until golden and blistered. Transfer the eggs to a plate lined with kitchen paper to drain.

3.   Pour out all but 15 ml/1 tbsp of oil from the wok. Stir in the sugar and fish sauce and simmer, stirring, until the sauce is thick.

4.   Arrange the eggs on a warmed serving plate and pour over the sauce. Sprinkle with the chopped chilli pepper and spring onions and garnish with the coriander.

Serves 4

6 | Crispy Tofu

Ingredients

25 g/1 oz/¼ cup rice flour
45 ml/3 tbsp cornflour
225 g/8 oz tofu, cut into strips
Oil for deep-frying
½ lettuce, shredded
Few sprigs fresh coriander
150 ml/¼ pt/⅔ cup Peanut Sauce (page 150)

Method

1. Mix together the rice flour and cornflour. Coat the tofu strips in the mixture until thoroughly covered then shake off any excess.

2. Heat the oil and deep-fry the tofu strips, in batches if necessary, for about 8 minutes until golden brown. Drain on kitchen paper.

3. Arrange on a warmed serving plate on a bed of lettuce and garnish with the coriander. Serve with the peanut sauce.

Serves 4

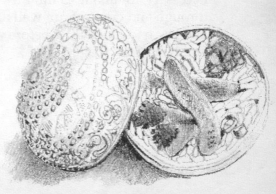

7 Fried Chicken Drumsticks

Ingredients

450 g/1 lb chicken drumsticks
4 cloves garlic, chopped
1 stick lemon grass, finely chopped
30 ml/2 tbsp fish sauce
15 ml/1 tbsp vegetable oil
15 ml/1 tbsp rice flour
5 ml/1 tsp soft brown sugar
5 ml/1 tsp chopped fresh coriander
Freshly ground black pepper
Oil for deep-frying

Method

1.   Place the chicken in a bowl. Mix together the remaining ingredients and season with pepper. Pour over the chicken, stir well, cover and refrigerate overnight.

2.   Heat the oil and deep-fry the chicken, in batches if necessary, for about 15 minutes until cooked through and crisp. Drain well on kitchen paper and leave to cool a little before serving with Chilli and Nut Sauce (page 144).

Serves 4

8 Kebabs with Peanut Sauce

Ingredients

45 ml/3 tbsp vegetable oil
2 cloves garlic, chopped
1 red chilli pepper, chopped
1 stick lemon grass, chopped
15 ml/1 tbsp curry powder
5 ml/1 tsp honey
5 ml/1 tsp fish sauce
225 g/8 oz chicken breast fillet, cut into strips
225 g/8 oz lean pork or beef, cut into strips
150 ml/1/4 pt/2/3 cup Peanut Sauce (page 150)

Method

1. Blend together the oil, garlic, chilli pepper, lemon grass, curry powder, honey and fish sauce in a blender or food processor.

2. Place the chicken and pork or beef in a bowl, pour over the marinade, cover and leave to marinate for about 4 hours.

3. Thread the meat on to skewers and grill under a preheated grill for about 15 minutes until the meat is cooked. Serve with peanut sauce.

Serves 4

9 | Thai Meatballs

Ingredients

100 g/4 oz minced beef
100 g/4 oz minced pork
Freshly ground black pepper
3 spring onions, chopped
4 cloves garlic, crushed
2.5 ml/ 1/2 tsp grated nutmeg
30 ml/2 tbsp fish sauce
30 ml/2 tbsp chopped fresh coriander
2 eggs, beaten
30 ml/2 tbsp plain flour
Oil for deep-frying

Method

1. Mix together the meats and season generously
    with pepper. Mix in the spring onions, garlic,
    nutmeg, fish sauce and coriander then bind
    together with the egg. Shape into small balls and
    lightly dust with flour.

2. Heat the oil and fry the balls for a few minutes
    until golden brown. Drain on kitchen paper and
    serve with Hot Chilli Sauce (page 143) or Chilli and
    Nut Sauce (page 144).

Serves 4

10 | Beef Satay

Ingredients

400 ml/14 fl oz/1 ¾ cups coconut cream
5 ml/1 tsp fish sauce
5 ml/1 tsp curry powder
5 ml/1 tsp turmeric
5 ml/1 tsp grated ginger root
450 g/1 lb steak, cut into strips

Method

1. Mix together the coconut cream, fish sauce, curry powder, turmeric and ginger. Add the meat and stir to coat thoroughly. Cover and chill overnight.

2. Thread the beef strips on to skewers and grill under a preheated grill for about 5 minutes each side. Serve with Cucumber Salad (page 114).

Serves 4

Soups

*Thais often start breakfast or a
light meal with a soup and many
have a wonderful spicy flavour
which whets the appetite for the
meal to follow. At a main meal,
the soups are served with the
other courses, rather than before.*

Chicken and Rice Soup

Ingredients

225 g/8 oz chicken, minced
1.2 l/2 pts/5 cups chicken stock
350 g/12 oz cooked long-grain rice
30 ml/2 tbsp fish sauce
5 ml/1 tsp chopped ginger root
2 shallots, chopped
Freshly ground black pepper
30 ml/2 tbsp groundnut oil
6 cloves garlic, chopped

Method

1. Form the chicken into small balls. Bring the stock to the boil and stir in the rice, fish sauce, ginger and shallots. Season with pepper. Drop in the chicken balls and simmer for about 10 minutes until the chicken is cooked through.

2. Meanwhile, heat the oil and fry the garlic until lightly browned.

3. Transfer the soup to a warmed soup tureen or individual bowls and spoon the garlic and oil sauce over the top.

Serves 4

2 Ginger Chicken Soup

Ingredients

600 ml/1 pt/2 ¹/₂ cups coconut milk
300 ml/¹/₂ pt/1 ¹/₄ cups water
225 g/8 oz chicken breast fillet, cut into strips
2.5 cm/1 in piece root ginger, sliced
45 ml/3 tbsp lemon juice
30 ml/2 tbsp fish sauce
4 spring onions, chopped
15 ml/1 tbsp chopped fresh coriander or parsley
1 red chilli pepper, chopped

Method

1. Bring the coconut milk and water to the boil, add the chicken and simmer gently for 10 minutes until the chicken is just cooked.

2. Add the ginger, lemon juice and fish sauce and simmer for a further 5 minutes.

3. Transfer to a serving bowl and sprinkle with the spring onions and coriander or parsley and serve garnished with chilli pepper.

Serves 4

3 Lemon Chicken and Vegetable Soup

Ingredients

750 ml/1 ¼ pts/3 cups chicken stock
1 stem lemon grass, chopped
1 chicken breast, skinned and coarsely chopped
225 g/8 oz cauliflower florets
1 tomato, skinned and cut into wedges
100 g/4 oz mushrooms, sliced
30 ml/2 tbsp fish sauce
15 ml/1 tbsp lemon juice
5 ml/1 tsp sugar

Method

1. Bring the stock to the boil in a large saucepan. Add the lemon grass and simmer for 5 minutes.

2. Add the chicken, cauliflower, tomato and mushrooms and simmer for 10 minutes until the chicken is cooked and the vegetables are just tender.

3. Stir in the fish sauce, lemon juice and sugar and simmer for 2 minutes. Serve accompanied by boiled or steamed rice.

Serves 4

Hot and Sour Prawn and Vegetable Soup

Ingredients

4 dried red chilli peppers
900 ml/1 ¹/2 pts/3 ³/4 cups chicken stock
1 onion
100 g/4 oz cod fillet
1 clove garlic
2 shallots
Salt
5 ml/1 tsp tamarind paste
90 ml/6 tbsp fish sauce
5 ml/1 tsp sugar
225 g/8 oz cooked prawns
450 g/1 lb beansprouts

Method

1.   Soak the chilli peppers in warm water for about 15 minutes. Drain, remove the stems and seeds and set aside.

2.   Bring the stock to the boil with the onion. Add the cod and simmer gently for 15 minutes. Strain the stock into a clean pan. Discard the onion.

3.   Blend the fish with the chilli peppers, garlic and shallots until smooth, adding a little stock if necessary. Season with salt. Stir the mixture into the stock. Mix the tamarind paste with a little hot water and stir it into the soup with the fish sauce and sugar. Bring to the boil and simmer for 4 minutes.

4.   Add the prawns and beansprouts, return to the boil then serve immediately.

Serves 4

5 | Corn and Prawn Soup

Ingredients

15 ml/1 tbsp vegetable oil
4 cloves garlic, crushed
2 shallots, finely chopped
900 ml/1 1/2 pts/3 3/4 cups chicken stock
30 ml/2 tbsp fish sauce
225 g/8 oz cooked prawns
300 g/11 oz canned creamed sweetcorn
Freshly ground black pepper
1 egg, beaten
15 ml/1 tbsp chopped fresh coriander

Method

1. Heat the oil and fry the garlic and shallots for about 4 minutes until lightly browned. Add the stock, fish sauce, prawns and corn and season with pepper. Bring to the boil and simmer for 2 minutes.

2. Stir the soup round with a fork as you gradually pour in the beaten egg, stirring continuously. Simmer for 1 minute. Serve garnished with coriander.

Serves 4

6   Fish Soup

Ingredients

6 shallots
5 green chilli peppers
1.5 l/2 ½ pts/6 cups chicken stock
3 stalks lemon grass, sliced
15 ml/1 tbsp grated ginger root
4 lime leaves
1 kg/2 lb cod or bass, cut into thick steaks
120 ml/4 fl oz/ ½ cup lime juice
45 ml/3 tbsp fish sauce
1 bunch fresh coriander, chopped

Method

1.   Leaving the skins intact, grill the shallots for about 10 minutes and the chilli peppers for about 5 minutes until charred on the outside and slightly tender. Remove the skins, crush slightly and put aside.

2.   Bring the chicken stock, lemon grass, ginger, lime leaves and coriander to the boil in a heavy-based saucepan. Add the fish and bring back to the boil. Remove from the heat.

3.   Add the shallots and chilli peppers, lime juice and fish sauce. Garnish with the coriander and serve at once.

Serves 4

7 **Prawn and Mushroom Soup**

Ingredients

750 ml/1 ¼ pts/3 cups chicken stock
100 g/4 oz broccoli florets
100 g/4 oz cabbage, shredded
100 g/4 oz mushrooms, sliced
6 spring onions, chopped
450 g/1 lb peeled prawns
15 ml/1 tbsp fish sauce
Freshly ground black pepper

Method

1. Bring the stock to the boil in a large saucepan. Add the broccoli, cabbage and mushrooms. If you are using uncooked prawns, add them as well. Simmer over a medium heat for about 4 minutes.

2. Add the spring onions, cooked prawns, if you are using them and fish sauce. Season with pepper and simmer for 1 minute. Serve hot with a steamed or boiled rice dish.

Serves 4

Seafood

*Seafood dishes are particularly
popular in southern Thailand
and there are many delicious
recipes. If the type of fish in the
recipe is unavailable, simply
substitute a similar fish.*

Bass with Ginger Sauce

Ingredients

10 dried Chinese mushrooms
60 ml/4 tbsp white wine vinegar
50 g/2 oz/¼ cup soft brown sugar
150 ml/¼ pt/ ⅔ cup water
45 ml/3 tbsp soy sauce
15 ml/1 tbsp chopped ginger root
3 spring onions, sliced
15 ml/1 tbsp cornflour
Juice of 1 lime
1 large sea bass, cleaned and gutted
Salt
30 ml/2 tbsp plain flour
Oil for frying
15 ml/1 tbsp chopped fresh coriander

Method

1. Soak the mushrooms in hot water for about 20 minutes. Drain. Discard the stems and chop the mushroom caps.

2. Mix together the mushrooms, wine vinegar, sugar, water and soy sauce and bring to the boil, stirring. Add the ginger and spring onions and stir-fry for 3 minutes. Mix the cornflour with the lime juice and 15 ml/1 tbsp of water and mix this into the sauce, stirring until the sauce thickens and becomes syrupy. Remove from the heat.

3. Trim the fish and rub it inside and out with salt. Dust lightly with flour. Heat the oil in a wok until almost smoking and fry the fish for about 3 minutes on each side until golden brown. Transfer

to a serving plate and pour over the sauce. Serve garnished with coriander.

Serves 6

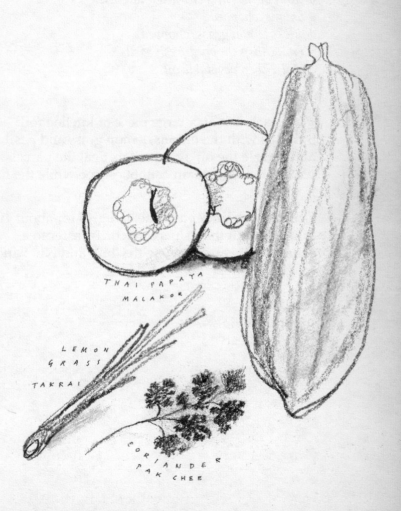

THAI PAPAYA
MALAKOR

LEMON
GRASS
TAKRAI

CORIANDER
PAK CHEE

2 | Baked Fish Parcels

Ingredients

4 trout or herring, cleaned and gutted
4 onions, chopped
4 sticks lemon grass, chopped
30 ml/2 tbsp chopped fresh basil
30 ml/2 tbsp vegetable oil

Method

1. Place each fish on a large piece of kitchen foil. Sprinkle with the onions, lemon grass and basil and drizzle the oil over the top. Seal the parcels well so that the steam cannot escape while the fish is cooking.

2. Grill the fish under a preheated grill for about 10 minutes until the fish is cooked. Transfer to a serving plate and serve with Chilli and Nut Sauce (page 144).

Serves 4

3 Mackerel with Garlic

Ingredients

4 cloves garlic, chopped
5 ml/1 tsp salt
Freshly ground white pepper
45 ml/3 tbsp vegetable oil
4 mackerel, filleted

Method

1. Mix together the garlic, salt, pepper and oil and rub it into the mackerel on all sides. Arrange in a shallow ovenproof dish, cover and chill for 2 hours.

2. Grill the mackerel under a preheated grill for about 5 minutes each side until the fish is cooked and golden brown, basting occasionally with a little more oil if necessary. Serve with Lime Sauce (page 146).

Serves 4

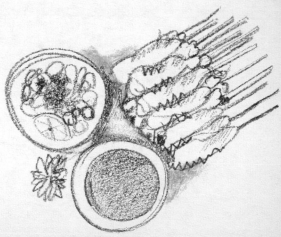

4 Thai Fried Herring

Ingredients

4 herrings, cleaned and gutted
15 ml/1 tbsp sea salt
5 ml/1 tsp turmeric
120 ml/4 fl oz/ 1/2 cup vegetable oil

Method

1. Trim the fish and clean well under running water. Pat dry.

2. Mix together the salt and turmeric and rub into the fish inside and out.

3. Heat the oil and fry the fish for a few minutes each side until crisp and golden brown. Drain on kitchen paper and serve with Hot Chilli Sauce (page 143).

Serves 4

5 Sole in Tamarind Sauce

Ingredients

150 ml/ 1/4 pt/ 2/3 cup groundnut oil
900 g/2 lb sole fillets
4 cloves garlic, crushed
45 ml/3 tbsp soy sauce
30 ml/2 tbsp soft brown sugar
15 ml/1 tbsp fish sauce
5 ml/1 tsp tamarind paste
75 ml/6 tbsp hot water
4 spring onions, chopped
15 ml/1 tbsp chopped ginger root
15 ml/1 tbsp chopped fresh coriander

Method

1. Heat the oil in a wok and fry the fillets for a few minutes on each side until golden brown. Drain on kitchen paper and arrange on a warmed serving plate.

2. Drain off most of the oil, add the garlic and fry until lightly browned. Stir in the soy sauce, sugar and fish sauce. Mix the tamarind paste with the water until smooth and stir into the pan. Stir-fry for 2 minutes. Add the spring onions and ginger and stir-fry for 2 minutes.

3. Spoon the sauce over the fish and serve garnished with coriander.

Serves 4

6 Fish Curry

Ingredients

15 ml/1 tbsp vegetable oil
45 ml/3 tbsp Green Curry Paste (page 154)
30 ml/2 tbsp fish sauce
600 ml/1 pt/2 ½ cups coconut cream
15 ml/1 tbsp cornflour
1 egg, beaten
3 spring onions, sliced
5 ml/1 tsp grated lemon rind
900 g/2 lb white fish fillets, sliced
30 ml/2 tbsp chopped fresh basil

Method

1. Heat the oil and fry the curry paste for 2 minutes, stirring continuously. Add the fish sauce, coconut cream, cornflour, egg, spring onions and lemon rind and cook for 3 minutes, stirring well until the sauce thickens.

2. Add the fish and simmer very gently for about 10 minutes until the fish is cooked, stirring occasionally. Serve sprinkled with basil.

Serves 4

7 | Sweet Seafood Curry

Ingredients

12 mussels, scrubbed and bearded
15 ml/1 tbsp vegetable oil
30 ml/2 tbsp Red Curry Paste (page 153)
15 ml/1 tbsp sugar
30 ml/2 tbsp fish sauce
600 ml/1 pt/2 1/2 cups coconut milk
450 ml/ 3/4 pt/2 cups chicken stock
450 g/1 lb cooked peeled prawns
225 g/8 oz pineapple, cut into chunks

Method

1.   Place the mussels in a heavy-based saucepan with a little water. Cover and heat over a medium heat for about 5 minutes, shaking the pan occasionally, until the mussels open. Discard any that remain closed. Shell the mussels and leave to one side.

2.   Heat the oil and fry the curry paste, sugar, fish sauce and half the coconut milk for 2 minutes until well blended. Leave over a medium heat for about 15 minutes until reduced to a thick paste, stirring occasionally.

3.   Stir in the remaining coconut milk and simmer until reduced again, stirring occasionally.

4.   Stir in the stock and reduce again.

5.   Stir in the mussels, prawns and pineapple and stir-fry for about 2 minutes until heated through. Serve at once.

Serves 4

8 | Prawn and Basil Stir-Fry

Ingredients

10 basil leaves
45 ml/3 tbsp vegetable oil
1 onion, chopped
1 clove garlic, chopped
2 green chilli peppers, seeded
100 g/4 oz mushrooms, sliced
450 g/1 lb peeled prawns
15 ml/1 tbsp fish sauce
5 ml/1 tsp sugar

Method

1. Soak the basil leaves in hot water for 20 minutes then drain well.

2. Heat the oil in a wok and stir-fry the onion, garlic, chilli peppers and mushrooms for 2 minutes until just soft.

3. Add the prawns, fish sauce, sugar and basil and stir-fry for about 4 minutes until heated through and well combined. Serve hot with a rice dish.

Serves 4

9 Prawns with Asparagus

Ingredients

25 g/1 oz dried Chinese mushrooms
450 g/1 lb asparagus
225 g/8 oz peeled prawns
45 ml/3 tbsp vegetable oil
3 cloves garlic, crushed
2 red chilli peppers, chopped
45 ml/3 tbsp oyster sauce

Method

1.   Soak the mushrooms in hot water for 30 minutes. Drain and discard the stems.

2.   Steam the mushrooms with the asparagus and prawns for about 10 minutes until tender. Arrange on a warmed serving plate and keep them warm.

3.   Meanwhile, heat the oil and fry the garlic and peppers for a few minutes until golden brown. Stir in the oyster sauce and pour over the prawns and vegetables.

Serves 4

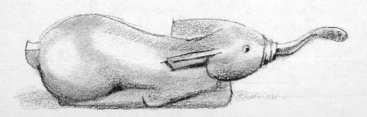

10 Prawns and Squid with Basil

Ingredients

450 g/1 lb squid
30 ml/2 tbsp vegetable oil
1 clove garlic, chopped
2 red chilli peppers, chopped
100 g/4 oz canned bamboo shoots, drained and sliced
5 ml/1 tsp cayenne pepper
2 shallots, chopped
45 ml/3 tbsp oyster sauce
A pinch of sugar
Freshly ground black pepper
100 g/4 oz cooked prawns
30 ml/2 tbsp chopped fresh basil

Method

1. To prepare the squid, pull the tentacles away from the body and remove and discard the skin. Cut off the plastic-like quill, the eyes and beak. Cut the squid into rings. Blanch in boiling water for about 2 minutes.

2. Heat the oil and fry the garlic and chilli peppers until lightly browned. Add the bamboo shoots, cayenne pepper and shallots and stir-fry for 3 minutes. Add the oyster sauce, season with a little sugar and pepper. Add the squid, prawns and basil and stir-fry for 3 minutes. Serve at once.

Serves 4

11 | Hot Chilli Prawns

Ingredients

75 ml/5 tbsp vegetable oil
10 ml/2 tsp chilli paste
450 g/1 lb peeled prawns
30 ml/2 tbsp fish sauce
5 ml/1 tsp soft brown sugar
2 sprigs fresh coriander

Method

1.   Heat the oil then stir in the chilli paste, using a quantity to suit your personal taste.

2.   Add the prawns, fish sauce and brown sugar and stir-fry for about 5 minutes.

3.   Remove the leaves from the coriander and stir them into the pan. Serve at once.

Serves 4

12 Scallops with Basil

Ingredients

225 g/8 oz shelled scallops
30 ml/2 tbsp vegetable oil
4 cloves garlic, crushed
50 g/2 oz mushrooms, sliced
50 g/2 oz canned bamboo shoots, drained and sliced
3 red chilli peppers, chopped
45 ml/3 tbsp oyster sauce
30 ml/2 tbsp chopped fresh basil
50 g/2 oz white cabbage, shredded

Method

1. Score the scallops a few times on the surface. Heat the oil and fry the garlic for 1 minute.

2. Add the scallops, mushrooms, bamboo shoots, chilli peppers and oyster sauce and stir-fry for about 6 minutes until the scallops are cooked.

3. Stir in the basil and stir-fry for 1 minute.

4. Arrange the cabbage round the edge of a serving plate and spoon the scallops and sauce into the centre.

Serves 4

13 | Clams with Ginger

Ingredients

900 g/2 lb clams, scrubbed
30 ml/2 tbsp water
15 ml/1 tbsp vegetable oil
3 cloves garlic, chopped
1 onion, sliced
1 red chilli pepper, chopped
2 spring onions, sliced
30 ml/2 tbsp chopped ginger root
30 ml/2 tbsp oyster sauce

Method

1.   Place all the ingredients in a large saucepan, cover
       and steam for about 5 minutes, shaking the pan
       occasionally, until the clams open. Discard any that
       do not open. Serve at once.

       Serves 4

14 Mussels with Chilli Peppers

Ingredients

60 ml/4 tbsp vegetable oil
6 shallots, chopped
4 cloves garlic, chopped
225 g/8 oz shelled mussels
4 red chilli peppers
15 ml/1 tbsp yellow bean sauce
15 ml/1 tbsp cornflour
60 ml/4 tbsp water
2 sprigs coriander

Method

1. Heat the oil and fry the shallots and garlic for about 5 minutes until lightly browned. Add the mussels, chilli peppers and yellow bean sauce and stir-fry for 5 minutes.

2. Mix together the cornflour and water and stir into the pan. Continue to stir over a low heat until the sauce thickens. Serve garnished with coriander.

Serves 4

Poultry

*Chicken is popular in Thailand
and is transformed into many
wonderful dishes, notably
delicious mellow curries.*

1 Thai Chicken Curry

Ingredients

4 chicken portions, boned and cut into bite-sized pieces
5 ml/1 tsp garam masala
2.5 ml/¹/₂ tsp salt
2.5 ml/¹/₂ tsp grated lemon rind
Pinch of ground cardamom
45 ml/3 tbsp vegetable oil
1 onion, cut into chunks
¹/₂ stick cinnamon
2 potatoes, cut into chunks
450 ml/ ³/₄ pt/2 cups coconut milk
1 bay leaf
30 ml/2 tbsp fish sauce
5 ml/1 tsp lemon juice
5 ml/1 tsp sugar
Pinch of chilli powder
50 g/2 oz roasted peanuts

Method

1. Place the chicken in a bowl. Mix together the garam masala, salt, lemon rind and cardamom and rub into the chicken.

2. Heat the oil and fry the onion with the cinnamon for 5 minutes until lightly browned.

3. Add the chicken mixture and fry until lightly browned on all sides.

4. Add the potatoes, coconut milk and bay leaf, cover and simmer for about 15 minutes until the potatoes are tender and the chicken is cooked.

5. Stir together the fish sauce, lemon juice, sugar and chilli powder. Stir into the pan and simmer, stirring continuously for about 5 minutes.

6.   Transfer to a warmed serving dish, remove the bay leaf and cinnamon and serve garnished with peanuts.

Serves 4

2 Panaeng Chicken Curry

Ingredients

450 ml/ ³/₄ pt/2 cups coconut milk
450 g/1 lb chicken, cut into chunks
1 clove garlic, finely chopped
1 dried red chilli pepper, chopped
2 spring onions, chopped
1 stalk lemon grass, chopped
30 ml/2 tbsp fish sauce
30 ml/2 tbsp peanut butter
15 ml/1 tbsp sugar
2.5 ml/ ¹/₂ tsp grated lemon rind
Pinch of ground coriander
Salt and freshly ground black pepper

Method

1.   Bring the coconut milk to the boil in a large
     saucepan then simmer for 15 minutes, stirring
     occasionally.

2.   Add the chicken, garlic, chilli pepper, onions and
     lemon grass, stir well, cover and simmer for 15
     minutes.

3.   Add the remaining ingredients and season with
     salt and pepper. Cover again and simmer gently
     for about 1 hour, stirring occasionally, until chicken
     is tender. Serve with a rice dish.

Serves 4

3 Grilled Chicken

Ingredients

4 chicken portions
1 clove garlic, chopped
30 ml/2 tbsp soy sauce
30 ml/2 tbsp fish sauce
15 ml/1 tbsp sugar
5 ml/1 tsp freshly ground black pepper
2 sprigs parsley
150 ml/ ^{1}/$_4$ pt/ ^{2}/$_3$ cup Sweet and Sour Sauce (page 148)

Method

1. Place the chicken portions in a large bowl. Mix together all the remaining ingredients except the parsley and sweet and sour sauce and pour over the chicken. Stir well to make sure it is well coated in the marinade. Cover and refrigerate for at least 5 hours.

2. Remove the chicken from the marinade and grill under a preheated grill for about 45 minutes until the chicken is tender, turning frequently and basting with any remaining marinade.

3. Transfer to a warmed serving plate, garnish with the parsley and serve with the sweet and sour sauce.

Serves 4

Chicken with Water Chestnuts

Ingredients

45 ml/3 tbsp vegetable oil
3 cloves garlic, crushed
5 ml/1 tsp ground coriander
Salt and freshly ground black pepper
450 g/1 lb chicken, chopped
3 chicken livers, chopped
450 ml/ 3/4 pt/2 cups chicken stock
225 g/8 oz canned water chestnuts, drained and sliced
15 ml/1 tbsp soft brown sugar

Method

1. Heat the oil, add the garlic and coriander and season with salt and pepper. Fry for 3 minutes, stirring well. Add the chicken and stir-fry for 3 minutes until golden brown. Add the chicken livers and stock, bring to the boil and simmer for 5 minutes.

2. Stir in the water chestnuts and sugar and season again with salt and pepper. Cover and simmer for about 10 minutes until the chicken is tender.

Serves 4

5 Chicken with Cashew Nuts

Ingredients

60 ml/4 tbsp vegetable oil
3 dried red chilli peppers
3 cloves garlic, crushed
450 g/1 lb chicken breast fillet, sliced
30 ml/2 tbsp oyster sauce
10 spring onions, chopped
225 g/8 oz/2 cups cashew nuts
1/2 lettuce, shredded

Method

1. Heat the oil and fry the chilli peppers whole for about 4 minutes. Remove them from the pan.

2. Add the garlic to the pan and stir-fry for 1 minute. Add the chicken and oyster sauce and stir-fry for about 5 minutes until the chicken is almost cooked. Add the onions and nuts and stir-fry for a further 2 minutes until the chicken is cooked and the ingredients are heated through.

3. Arrange the lettuce around a warmed serving plate and spoon over the chicken mixture. Serve at once.

Serves 4

6 Chicken with Bamboo Shoots

Ingredients

30 ml/2 tbsp vegetable oil
2 cloves garlic, crushed
3 chilli peppers, chopped
1 red pepper, chopped
350 g/12 oz chicken, chopped
100 g/4 oz canned bamboo shoots, drained and sliced
30 ml/2 tbsp oyster sauce
5 ml/1 tsp sugar
Freshly ground black pepper
30 ml/2 tbsp chopped fresh basil

Method

1. Heat the oil and fry the garlic, chilli peppers and pepper until lightly browned. Add the chicken and stir-fry for a few minutes until lightly browned. Add the bamboo shoots, oyster sauce and sugar and season with pepper. Stir-fry for about 5 minutes until the chicken is tender. Stir in the basil and serve at once.

Serves 4

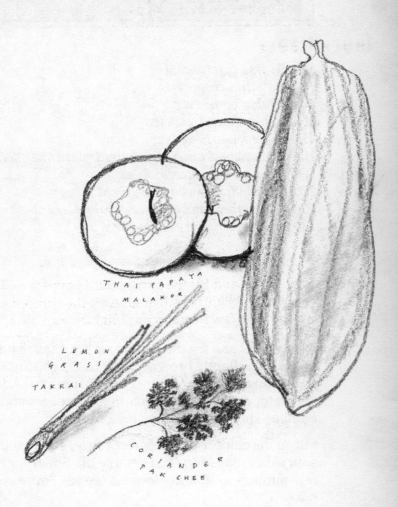

THAI PAPAYA
MALAKOR

LEMON
GRASS
TAKRAI

CORIANDER
PAK CHEE

7 Sweet and Sour Chicken

Ingredients

30 ml/2 tbsp vegetable oil
2 cloves garlic, chopped
15 ml/1 tbsp bean sauce
350 g/12 oz chicken, chopped
4 spring onions, sliced
100 g/4 oz canned water chestnuts, drained and sliced
100 g/4 oz baby sweetcorn, sliced
100 g/4 oz button mushrooms, sliced
75 g/3 oz canned bamboo shoots, drained and sliced
120 ml/4 fl oz/ 1/2 cup chicken stock
30 ml/2 tbsp oyster sauce
30 ml/2 tbsp Sweet and Sour Sauce (page 148)
5 ml/1 tsp soy sauce
5 ml/1 tsp sesame oil

Method

1. Heat the oil and fry the garlic and bean sauce until the garlic is lightly browned. Stir in the chicken and spring onions and stir-fry for 2 minutes. Add the water chestnuts, sweetcorn, mushrooms and bamboo shoots and stir-fry for 2 minutes.

2. Stir in the chicken stock, oyster sauce, sweet and sour sauce, soy sauce and sesame oil. Stir-fry for a few minutes until the chicken is tender. Serve at once.

Serves 4

8 Stuffed Omelette

Ingredients

4 cloves garlic, chopped
2.5 ml/ ¹/₂ tsp ground coriander
Freshly ground black pepper
45 ml/3 tbsp vegetable oil
100 g/4 oz chicken, minced
1 onion, chopped
100 g/4 oz mangetout, chopped
1 tomato, skinned and chopped
5 ml/1 tsp sugar
8 eggs, beaten
15 ml/1 tbsp fish sauce
15 ml/1 tbsp chopped fresh coriander

Method

1. Crush the garlic with the coriander and season well with pepper. Heat half the oil and fry the garlic mixture until lightly browned. Add the chicken and stir-fry until lightly browned. Stir in the onion, mangetout, tomato and sugar and stir-fry for 3 minutes.

2. Beat the eggs with the fish sauce. Heat half the remaining oil in a frying pan and fry half the eggs until golden brown on the underside. Spoon half the chicken mixture into the centre of the omelette, fold it in half and fry for 1 minute. Transfer to a warmed serving plate and fry the second omelette. Arrange on the serving plate and serve sprinkled with coriander.

Serves 4

9 Grilled Quail

Ingredients

30 ml/2 tbsp chopped ginger root
6 cloves garlic, chopped
1 stick lemon grass, chopped
300 ml/½ pt/1 ¼ cups coconut milk
45 ml/3 tbsp oyster sauce
15 ml/1 tbsp curry powder
15 ml/1 tbsp soft brown sugar
15 ml/1 tbsp sesame oil
5 ml/1 tsp soy sauce
8 quail
45 ml/3 tbsp vegetable oil
Salt and freshly ground black pepper

Method

1.   Mix together the ginger, 2 cloves of garlic, the
      lemon grass and a little coconut milk and pound or
      blend to a smooth paste. Mix in the remaining
      coconut milk, the oyster sauce, curry powder,
      sugar, sesame oil and soy sauce. Pour over the
      quail, cover and chill overnight, turning
      occasionally.

2.   Bake the quail in a preheated oven at 240°C/
      475°F/gas mark 9 for about 10 minutes until
      partly cooked.

3.   Meanwhile, heat the oil and fry the remaining
      garlic until lightly browned. Season well with salt
      and pepper.

4.   Spoon the oil carefully over the quail and continue
      to cook for a further 10 minutes until the quail are
      cooked.

Serves 4

10 Duck with Ginger and Garlic

Ingredients

2 red chilli peppers, chopped
3 cloves garlic, crushed
15 ml/1 tbsp vegetable oil
15 ml/1 tbsp soft brown sugar
10 ml/2 tsp soy sauce
5 ml/1 tsp sesame oil
5 ml/1 tsp grated ginger root
5 ml/1 tsp honey
5 ml/1 tsp lemon juice
5 ml/1 tsp five-spice powder
1 duck

Method

1. Blend together all the spice ingredients in a blender or food processor. Rub the mixture all over the duck, inside and out.

2. Roast the duck in a preheated oven at 200°C/400°F/gas mark 6 for 30 minutes then reduce the temperature to 190°C/375°F/gas mark 5 for a further 1 hour or until the duck is cooked.

Serves 4

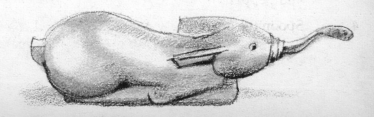

Roast Duck

Ingredients

2 *cloves garlic, chopped*
75 *ml/5 tbsp bean sauce*
75 *ml/5 tbsp hoisin sauce*
75 *ml/5 tbsp water*
60 *ml/4 tbsp soy sauce*
30 *ml/2 tbsp sherry*
15 *ml/1 tbsp soft brown sugar*
30 *ml/2 tbsp chopped ginger root*
5 *ml/1 tsp ground coriander*
1 *large duck*

Method

1. Mix together all the ingredients except the duck. Place the duck in a bowl, pour over the sauces and stir to coat well. Cover and leave to marinate in a cool place overnight, turning occasionally.

2. Drain the duck and roast breast side up in a preheated oven at 200°C/400°F/gas mark 6 for 30 minutes. Baste with the juices, turn the bird over, reduce the oven temperature to 180°C/350°F/gas mark 4 and roast for a further 30 minutes.

3. Baste the duck again and continue to cook until it is cooked through and crisp on the outside, draining off any juices if necessary. Serve with the remaining marinade as a dipping sauce.

Serves 4

Meat

*Many Thai main course dishes
are hot and spicy and sometimes
fairly dry. If you prefer a milder
sauce while you become
accustomed to the new flavours,
reduce the amount of the
seasoning ingredients and taste
as you cook to make sure the
sauce is not too hot.*

1 Thai Beef Curry

Ingredients

45 ml/3 tbsp vegetable oil
15 ml/1 tbsp Curry Paste (page 151)
450 g/1 lb lean beef, cubed
1 onion, sliced
1 red chilli pepper, chopped
1 potato, cubed
250 ml/8 fl oz/1 cup coconut milk
30 ml/2 tbsp fish sauce
5 ml/1 tsp soft brown sugar
15 ml/1 tbsp roasted peanuts

Method

1. Heat the oil and fry the curry paste for 2 minutes. Add the beef, onion, chilli pepper and potato and stir-fry for 5 minutes. Add the coconut milk, fish sauce and sugar and stir-fry for a further 5 minutes.

2. Cover the pan and leave to simmer over a gentle heat for about 20 minutes, stirring occasionally, until the ingredients are cooked and the sauce is thick. Serve sprinkled with peanuts.

Serves 4

2 Beef with Noodles

Ingredients

4 Chinese dried mushrooms
45 ml/3 tbsp vegetable oil
450 g/1 lb steak, thinly sliced
1 onion, thinly sliced
1 clove garlic, crushed
225 g/8 oz broccoli, chopped
5 ml/1 tsp cornflour (cornstarch)
60 ml/4 tbsp chicken stock
5 ml/1 tsp soy sauce
5 ml/1 tsp fish sauce
Freshly ground black pepper

Method

1. Soak the mushrooms in hot water for 30 minutes. Drain well, discard the stems and chop the mushrooms.

2. Heat most of the oil in a wok or frying pan and fry the steak over a high heat until browned on all sides. Remove from the pan.

3. Heat the remaining oil and fry the onion and garlic for about 2 minutes until just softened. Add the broccoli and stir well.

4. Mix together the cornflour and stock and add it to the pan. Bring to the boil, cover and simmer for about 4 minutes until the broccoli is just tender.

5. Add the mushrooms, soy sauce, fish sauce and beef. Season with pepper. Bring back to the boil and stir-fry for about 3 minutes until heated through. Serve hot with noodles.

Serves 4

3 Beef with Oyster Sauce

Ingredients

8 spring onions
25 g/1 oz Chinese dried mushrooms
30 ml/2 tbsp vegetable oil
3 cloves garlic, crushed
450 g/1 lb rump steak, cut into thin strips
45 ml/3 tbsp oyster sauce

Method

1. Trim the spring onions and slice them lengthways almost to the bulb into thin strips. Place in a bowl of iced water and chill while you prepare the dish so that they curl.

2. Soak the mushrooms in hot water for 30 minutes. Drain well. Discard the stems and slice the caps thinly.

3. Heat the oil and stir-fry the garlic for 1 minute. Add the steak and stir-fry for about 2 minutes over a high heat. Add the mushrooms and oyster sauce and stir-fry for a further 2 minutes.

4. Transfer to a serving plate and serve with the spring onions.

Serves 4

4 Hot Chilli Pork

Ingredients

45 ml/3 tbsp vegetable oil
1 onion, chopped
2 cloves garlic, chopped
350 g/12 oz lean pork, cubed
3 red chilli peppers, cut into strips
100 g/4 oz mushrooms, sliced
5 ml/1 tsp cornflour
30 ml/2 tbsp oyster sauce

Method

1. Heat the oil and fry the onion and garlic for about 5 minutes until lightly browned. Add the pork, peppers and mushrooms stir-fry for 3 minutes.

2. Mix the cornflour with the oyster sauce until smooth and stir it into the pan, adding a little water if the sauce is too thick. Stir-fry briefly until the ingredients are well combined and the pork is cooked. Serve at once.

Serves 4

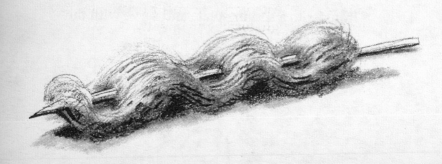

5 Pork Satay with Peanut Sauce

Ingredients

675 g/1 1/2 lb lean pork, cut into strips
30 ml/2 tbsp fish sauce
10 ml/2 tsp curry powder
10 ml/2 tsp sugar
Freshly ground black pepper
300 ml/1/2 pt/1 1/2 cups coconut milk
60 ml/4 tbsp crunchy peanut butter

Method

1. Place the pork in a large bowl. Mix together half the fish sauce, the curry powder and sugar and season with pepper. Pour over the pork and mix well. Cover and refrigerate for at least 5 hours.

2. To make the peanut sauce, mix together the coconut milk, peanut butter and remaining fish sauce. Bring to the boil, stirring constantly, then remove from the heat and leave to cool. Cover and refrigerate until ready to serve.

3. Thread the pork on to small skewers and grill under a preheated grill for about 10 minutes until cooked through, turning frequently.

4. Serve hot with the sauce.

Serves 4

6 Green Pork Curry

Ingredients

45 ml/3 tbsp vegetable oil
450 g/1 lb lean pork, cubed
150 ml/¼ pt/ ⅔ cup Green Curry Paste (page 154)
30 ml/2 tbsp fish sauce
15 ml/1 tbsp soft brown sugar
600 ml/1 pt/2½ cups coconut milk
45 ml/3 tbsp chopped fresh basil
1 red chilli pepper, cut into strips

Method

1. Heat the oil and fry the pork quickly until sealed on all sides. Remove from the pan.

2. Add the curry sauce, fish sauce and sugar to the pan and fry for a few minutes, stirring until the ingredients are well combined. Stir in one-third of the coconut milk, bring to the boil and simmer until reduced to a thick paste.

3. Stir in half the remaining coconut milk and reduce again.

4. Stir in the remaining coconut milk and return the pork to the pan. Simmer until the sauce is reduced and the pork is cooked, adding a little water to the sauce if the mixture becomes too dry.

5. Stir in the basil and stir-fry for 1 minute. Serve garnished with chilli peppers.

Serves 4

7 Quick Stir-Fried Pork

Ingredients

45 ml/3 tbsp vegetable oil
350 g/12 oz lean pork, cubed
2 cloves garlic, chopped
45 ml/3 tbsp light soy sauce
45 ml/3 tbsp fish sauce
45 ml/3 tbsp soft brown sugar
Freshly ground black pepper

Method

1. Heat the oil and fry the pork until sealed on all sides. Add the garlic and stir-fry for 2 minutes. Stir in the soy sauce, fish sauce and sugar and season with pepper. Stir-fry for a few minutes until the pork is cooked and the sauce is thick. Serve at once.

    Serves 4

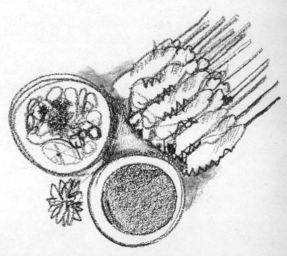

8 | Minced Pork and Prawns

Ingredients

300 ml/ ^{1}/$_2$ pt/1 ^{1}/$_4$ cups coconut milk
225 g/8 oz cooked peeled prawns, minced
225 g/8 oz pork, minced
2 red chilli peppers, chopped
Salt and freshly ground black pepper
5 ml/1 tsp sugar
15 ml/1 tbsp chopped fresh coriander

Method

1. Bring the coconut milk to a simmer. Mix together
    the prawns, pork and peppers and season with salt
    and pepper. Stir into the milk and return to the
    boil. Simmer for about 5 minutes, stirring
    occasionally. Stir in the sugar and coriander and
    season again with pepper to taste.

    Serves 4

9 Pork Omelette

Ingredients

8 eggs, beaten
30 ml/2 tbsp fish sauce
225 g/8 oz pork, minced
3 cloves garlic, chopped
4 shallots, finely chopped
15 ml/1 tbsp chopped fresh coriander
30 ml/2 tbsp vegetable oil
2 spring onions, sliced

Method

1. Beat together the eggs and fish sauce then mix in the pork, garlic, shallots and coriander.

2. Heat half the oil in an omelette pan and pour in half the mixture. Cook for a few minutes until golden brown on the underside then turn and cook the other side. Transfer to a warmed serving plate then repeat with the remaining oil and egg mixture.

3. Place the omelettes on top of each other, garnish with spring onions and serve at once.

Serves 4

10 | Thai Egg Rolls

Ingredients

4 Chinese dried mushrooms
100 g/4 oz transparent noodles
15 ml/1 tbsp vegetable oil
1 onion, chopped
1 clove garlic, chopped
225 g/8 oz minced beef
225 g/8 oz minced pork
2 carrots, grated
100 g/4 oz beansprouts
15 ml/1 tbsp fish sauce
5 ml/1 tsp sugar
Freshly ground black pepper
1 egg, beaten
450 g/1 lb won ton wrappers or filo pastry
50 g/2 oz/1/4 cup butter or margarine, melted
Oil for deep-frying

Method

1. Soak the mushrooms in hot water for 30 minutes. Drain, discard the stems and chop the caps.

2. Soak the noodles in hot water until soft. Drain and chop coarsely.

3. Heat the oil and fry the onion and garlic for about 5 minutes until soft but not browned. Add the pork and beef and fry until browned. Remove from the heat and stir in the carrots. Leave to cool.

4. Stir in the beansprouts, fish sauce, sugar and pepper and bind together with the egg.

5. If using filo pastry, cut it into 20 cm/8 in squares. Keep the remaining pastry or won ton

wrappers covered in a damp cloth while you are
working on one egg roll.

6.   Brush a square with butter or margarine and place
a little filling just below the centre. Fold up the
bottom edge over the filling. Fold in the two sides
to overlap then roll up towards the top, brushing
with a little more butter or margarine if necessary
to seal. Repeat with the remaining rolls.

7.   Heat the oil and fry the egg rolls, in batches if
necessary, for about 10 minutes until golden
brown. Serve hot with Spiced Fish Sauce (page 148)
or Sweet and Sour Sauce (page 148).

Serves 4

Vegetable Dishes

Stir-frying is the favourite method of cooking vegetables and vegetable dishes in Thailand as it retains their flavours and crisp texture. A wok is the best utensil to use, but if you do not have one, use a large saucepan instead.

Sweet and Sour Stir-Fry

Ingredients

30 ml/2 tbsp vegetable oil
1 onion, sliced
1 clove garlic, chopped
100 g/4 oz cauliflower florets
100 g/4 oz broccoli florets
100 g/4 oz green beans, sliced
100 g/4 oz mushrooms, sliced
30 ml/2 tbsp fish sauce
30 ml/2 tbsp tomato purée
30 ml/2 tbsp sugar
15 ml/1 tbsp cornflour
15 ml/1 tbsp water
Freshly ground black pepper

Method

1. Heat the oil in a wok until very hot. Add the onion and garlic and stir-fry for about 4 minutes until soft.

2. Add the cauliflower, broccoli and beans and stir-fry for 4 minutes.

3. Add the mushrooms and stir-fry for 1 minute.

4. Stir in the fish sauce, tomato purée and sugar and season with pepper. Mix together the cornflour and water and stir it into the pan. Season with pepper. Continue to stir-fry for a further few minutes until the vegetables are just tender. Serve with a rice dish.

Serves 4

2 Vegetables with Peanut Sauce

Ingredients

60 ml/4 tbsp vegetable oil
50 g/2 oz tofu, cubed
2 onions, sliced
$^1/_2$ iceberg lettuce
$^1/_2$ cucumber, sliced
2 tomatoes, sliced
100 g/4 oz beansprouts
150 ml/$^1/_4$ pt/$^2/_3$ cup Peanut Sauce (page 150)

Method

1. Heat the oil and fry the tofu and onions until lightly browned. Drain on kitchen paper.

2. Arrange the lettuce, cucumber, tomatoes and beansprouts in a salad bowl. Spoon the tofu and onions into the centre and serve with the peanut sauce.

Serves 4

3 Ginger Beans

Ingredients

> 225 g/8 oz green beans
> 30 ml/2 tbsp vegetable oil
> 3 red chilli peppers, chopped
> 15 ml/1 tbsp grated ginger root
> 5 ml/1 tsp grated lemon rind
> 150 ml/ ¼ pt/ ⅔ cup coconut milk
> 5 ml/1 tsp fish sauce
> 100 g/4 oz white cabbage, shredded

Method

1. Slice the beans diagonally into 2.5 cm/1 in pieces.

2. Heat the oil and fry the chilli peppers, ginger and lemon rind for 1 minute. Add the beans, coconut milk and fish sauce and stir-fry for 2 minutes.

3. Add the cabbage and stir-fry for 3 minutes until all the ingredients are just tender but still crisp.

Serves 4

4 | Broccoli Stir-Fry

Ingredients

450 g/1 lb broccoli florets
45 ml/3 tbsp vegetable oil
2 cloves garlic, chopped
15 ml/1 tbsp bean sauce
15 ml/1 tbsp oyster sauce
15 ml/1 tbsp soy sauce
15 ml/1 tbsp sugar

Method

1. Blanch the broccoli florets in boiling water for 30 seconds. Remove and drain.

2. Heat the oil and fry the garlic and bean sauce until the garlic is lightly browned. Add the broccoli, oyster sauce, soy sauce and sugar and stir-fry for a few minutes until the broccoli is well coated and slightly softened but still crisp.

Serves 4

5 | Fried Beansprouts

Ingredients

45 ml/3 tbsp vegetable oil
3 cloves garlic, chopped
225 g/8 oz pork, diced
100 g/4 oz cooked prawns
15 ml/1 tbsp fish sauce
5 ml/1 tsp sugar
Freshly ground black pepper
225 g/8 oz beansprouts

Method

1.　Heat the oil and fry the garlic until lightly browned. Add the pork and stir-fry for 2 minutes. Add the prawns and stir-fry for 1 minute. Stir in the fish sauce and sugar and season with pepper. Stir in the beansprouts and stir-fry for 2 minutes until tender but still crisp. Serve at once.

Serves 4

6 Stuffed Courgettes

Ingredients

4 large courgettes
225 g/8 oz pork, minced
2 cloves garlic, chopped
15 ml/1 tbsp fish sauce
Freshly ground black pepper
8 cooked, peeled prawns
2 sprigs coriander

Method

1. Slice the courgettes in half lengthways and scoop out the seeds to make a boat shape.

2. Mix together the pork, garlic and fish sauce and season with pepper. Spoon the mixture into the courgette shells and press down firmly. Arrange in a single layer in a steamer and steam over boiling water for about 20 minutes until the vegetables are tender and the pork is cooked.

3. Garnish with the prawns and coriander and serve at once.

Serves 4

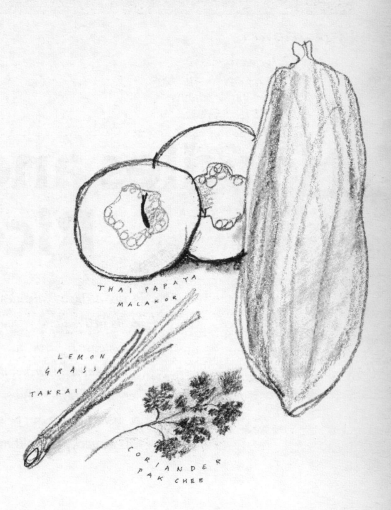

THAI PAPAYA
MALAKOR

LEMON
GRASS
TAKRAI

CORIANDER
PAK CHEE

Noodles and Rice

A rice dish accompanies most meals in Thailand, or you can choose to serve noodles to complement your main dish. There are also more substantial rice dishes which can be served as a snack or a light meal in themselves.

Egg Noodles with Thick Sauce

Ingredients

> 5 ml/1 tsp tamarind paste
> 15 ml/1 tbsp hot water
> 5 ml/1 tsp salt
> 100 g/4 oz soft brown sugar
> 90 ml/6 tbsp white wine vinegar
> 60 ml/4 tbsp water
> 350 g/12 oz egg noodles

Method

1. Mix the tamarind paste smoothly with the hot water then mix it with all the remaining ingredients except the noodles in a small saucepan. Bring to the boil then simmer for 10 minutes, stirring continuously and adding a little more water if necessary, until the sauce is thick and smooth.

2. Bring a saucepan of water to the boil, toss in the noodles and simmer for a few minutes until just tender. Drain well and arrange on a serving dish. Pour over the sauce and serve at once.

Serves 4

2   Mixed Vegetables Noodles

Ingredients

Oil for deep-frying
100 g/4 oz egg noodles
30 ml/2 tbsp vegetable oil
1 clove garlic, chopped
100 g/4 oz chicken, diced
50 g/2 oz canned bamboo shoots, drained and sliced
1 shallot, sliced
50 g/2 oz canned water chestnuts, drained and sliced
4 baby sweetcorn, halved
50 g/2 oz mushrooms, sliced
45 ml/3 tbsp oyster sauce
250 ml/8 fl oz/1 cup chicken stock
15 ml/1 tbsp cornflour
30 ml/2 tbsp Sweet and Sour Sauce (page 148)
A few drops of sesame oil

Method

1. Heat the oil and fry the egg noodles until golden brown. Drain well and arrange on a warmed serving plate.

2. Heat the oil and fry the garlic for 3 minutes until lightly browned. Add the chicken, bamboo shoots, shallot, water chestnuts, corn and mushrooms and stir-fry for 20 seconds. Add the oyster sauce and stock and bring to the boil. Mix the cornflour into the sweet and sour sauce, stir it into the pan and stir-fry for 30 seconds. Sprinkle with the sesame oil and spoon over the noodles. Serve at once.

Serves 4

3 Rice Noodles

Ingredients

750 ml/1 1/4 pts/3 cups water
350 g/12 oz rice noodles

Method

1. Bring the water to the boil in a large saucepan. Add the noodles and return to the boil.

2. Reduce the heat to medium and simmer for about 5 minutes until tender.

3. Drain well, rinse in cold water and serve at once.

Serves 4

Rice Noodles with Chicken

Ingredients

225 g/8 oz rice noodles
60 ml/4 tbsp vegetable oil
3 cloves garlic, chopped
100 g/4 oz chicken breast, sliced
1 egg, beaten
225 g/8 oz beansprouts
15 ml/1 tbsp tomato purée
30 ml/2 tbsp chopped peanuts
30 ml/2 tbsp fish sauce
30 ml/2 tbsp chopped fresh chives
5 ml/1 tsp soy sauce
5 ml/1 tsp sugar
1 lime, sliced

Method

1. Soak the noodles in warm water for 30 minutes. Drain well.

2. Heat the oil and fry the garlic until lightly browned. Stir in the chicken and egg and fry for 3 minutes. Stir in the noodles, beansprouts, tomato purée, peanuts, fish sauce, soy sauce and sugar and stir-fry for 5 minutes. Stir in the chives and mix well. Serve garnished with lime slices.

Serves 4

5 Rice Noodles with Broccoli

Ingredients

350 g/12 oz broccoli florets
75 ml/5 tbsp vegetable oil
225 g/8 oz rice noodles
4 cloves garlic, chopped
100 g/4 oz lean beef, cut into strips
15 ml/1 tbsp oyster sauce
10 ml/2 tsp yellow bean sauce
5 ml/1 tsp cornflour

Method

1. Blanch the broccoli in boiling water for 2 minutes. Drain well.

2. Heat 45 ml/3 tbsp of oil and fry the noodles for 3 minutes. Transfer to a warmed serving dish.

3. Heat the remaining oil and fry the garlic until lightly browned. Add the beef and broccoli and stir-fry for 2 minutes. Stir in the oyster sauce and yellow bean sauce and stir-fry for 2 minutes. Mix the cornflour with a little water, stir it into the pan and stir-fry for about 5 minutes. Spoon over the noodles and serve at once.

Serves 4

6 Thai Rice

Ingredients

450 g/1 lb/2 cups long-grain rice
600 ml/1 pt/2 ¹/₂ cups water

Method

1. Place the rice and water in a large saucepan and bring to the boil. Simmer for 3 minutes.

2. Cover the pan, reduce the heat and simmer for about 20 minutes until the rice is tender and the water has been absorbed.

3. Remove from the heat, leave covered and steam for 10 minutes.

4. Transfer to a warmed serving bowl and fluff the rice with a fork.

Serves 4

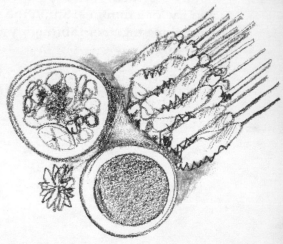

7 Red Fried Rice

Ingredients

6 spring onions
30 ml/2 tbsp vegetable oil
1 onion, chopped
3 cloves garlic, chopped
225 g/8 oz cooked prawns
30 ml/2 tbsp fish sauce
450 g/1 lb cooked rice, chilled
45 ml/3 tbsp tomato ketchup
1/2 cucumber, sliced

Method

1. Slice the spring onions lengthways almost to the bulb then leave them to soak in cold water so that they curl.

2. Heat the oil and fry the onion and garlic until lightly browned. Add the prawns and fish sauce and fry for 2 minutes. Stir in the rice and mix everything together thoroughly. Stir in the tomato ketchup.

3. Arrange the salad on a serving plate and garnish with the spring onions and cucumber slices.

Serves 4

8 Chilli Fried Rice

Ingredients

30 ml/2 tbsp vegetable oil
2 onions, chopped
2 red chilli peppers, chopped
15 ml/1 tbsp Red Curry Paste (page 153)
100 g/4 oz ham, diced
450 g/1 lb cooked rice, chilled
3 eggs, beaten
100 g/4 oz cooked prawns
45 ml/3 tbsp fish sauce
5 spring onions, chopped
15 ml/1 tbsp chopped fresh coriander

Method

1. Heat the oil and fry the onions and peppers for about 5 minutes until soft. Stir in the curry paste and fry for 4 minutes. Add the ham and stir-fry for 2 minutes. Add the rice and stir until the rice is well coated and heated through.

2. Make a well in the centre and pour in the eggs. Cook for 1 minute, then stir them into the rice. Stir in the prawns and fish sauce.

3. Transfer to a serving dish and garnish with the spring onions and coriander.

Serves 4

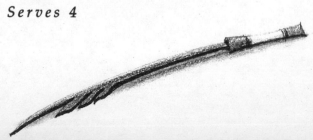

9 Beef Fried Rice

Ingredients

30 ml/2 tbsp vegetable oil
1 onion, chopped
1 clove garlic, chopped
225 g/8 oz beef, cut into strips
450 g/1 lb/2 cups cooked long-grain rice
200 g/7 oz canned tomatoes, chopped
15 ml/1 tbsp tomato purée
15 ml/1 tbsp fish sauce
2.5 ml/1/2 tsp cayenne pepper
1/2 cucumber, thinly sliced
3 spring onions, chopped
1 sprig flat-leaf parsley

Method

1. Heat the oil and fry the onion and garlic for about 4 minutes until just soft.

2. Increase the heat, add the beef and stir-fry for 5 minutes until the beef is cooked.

3. Add the rice, tomatoes, tomato purée, fish sauce and cayenne pepper and stir-fry for 4 minutes.

4. Transfer to a warmed serving plate and serve garnished with the cucumber, spring onions and parsley.

Serves 4

10 | Chicken Fried Rice

Ingredients

30 ml/2 tbsp vegetable oil
1 onion, chopped
1 clove garlic, crushed
100 g/4 oz chicken, diced
5 ml/1 tsp oyster sauce
1 egg, beaten
450 g/1 lb cooked rice
30 ml/2 tbsp fish sauce
5 ml/1 tsp sugar
5 ml/1 tsp tomato purée
2.5 ml/1/2 tsp light soy sauce
1 small tomato, cut into wedges
2 sprigs coriander
A few cucumber slices
Juice of 1/2 lime

Method

1. Heat the oil and fry the onion and garlic for about 5 minutes until lightly browned. Stir in the chicken and oyster sauce and stir-fry for 30 seconds. Add the egg and stir into the chicken mixture then add the rice and mix well.

2. Add the fish sauce, sugar, tomato purée, soy sauce and tomato and stir-fry for 3 minutes. Serve garnished with coriander and cucumber and sprinkled with lime juice.

Serves 4

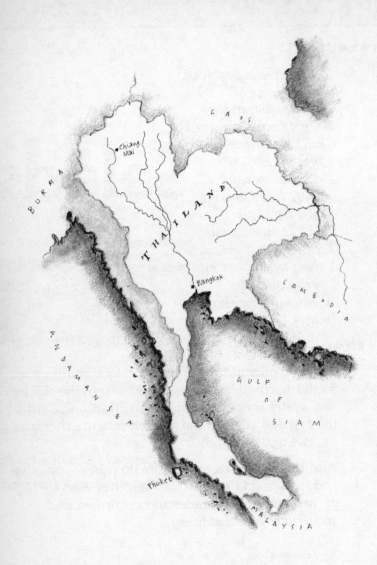

Salads

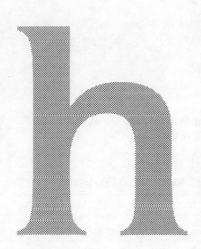

In Thailand, salads are composed of whatever ingredients are fresh and readily available – often harvested from the garden or picked from the countryside. It is not easy to create authentic Thai salads outside their native land, but you can conjure up delicious salads which have the flavour of Thailand and will perfectly complement your Thai meal.

1 Beef Salad

Ingredients

25 g/1 oz transparent noodles
450 g/1 lb cooked beef, cut into strips
1 onion, sliced
3 spring onions, chopped
$1/2$ cucumber, sliced
1 red chilli pepper, chopped
1 stick lemon grass, sliced
60 ml/4 tbsp lime juice
15 ml/1 tbsp fish sauce
30 ml/2 tbsp chopped fresh mint

Method

1. Soak the noodles in hot water for about 10 minutes. Drain and cut into pieces.

2. Mix the noodles with all the remaining ingredients and toss the ingredients together well. Chill before serving.

Serves 4-6

2 Cabbage Salad

Ingredients

1 small white cabbage
30 ml/2 tbsp groundnut oil
1 red onion, chopped
4 cloves garlic, crushed
100 g/4 oz cooked pork, chopped
5 ml/1 tsp salt
30 ml/2 tbsp fish sauce
Juice of 1 lime
15 ml/1 tbsp roasted peanuts, crushed
150 ml/ 1/4 pt/ 2/3 cup coconut cream
8 cooked peeled prawns

Method

1. Blanch the cabbage in boiling water for 3 minutes then drain and chop.

2. Heat the oil and fry the onion and garlic for about 5 minutes until lightly browned. Remove from the pan and leave to cool.

3. Toss together the pork, salt, fish sauce, lime juice, peanuts and coconut cream. Garnish with the prawns and fried onions and garlic.

Serves 4-6

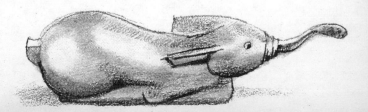

3 | Minted Chicken Salad

Ingredients

450 g/1 lb chicken, minced
1 stick lemon grass, chopped
3 red chilli peppers, chopped
45 ml/3 tbsp lime juice
15 ml/1 tbsp fish sauce
2 spring onions, chopped
30 ml/2 tbsp chopped fresh coriander
30 ml/2 tbsp chopped fresh mint
A few mint leaves
1 lettuce

Method

1. Heat a small frying pan and fry the chicken for a few minutes until cooked through, stirring continuously. Leave to cool.

2. Mix the chicken with all the remaining ingredients except the lettuce and mint leaves. Garnish with the mint leaves and serve on a bed of lettuce.

Serves 4

4 Chilli Pepper Salad

Ingredients

5 shallots
4 red chilli peppers
3 tomatoes
30 ml/2 tbsp fish sauce
30 ml/2 tbsp lime juice
5 ml/1 tsp sugar
1 crisp lettuce

Method

1. Without removing the skins, grill the shallots, peppers and tomatoes until slightly charred and beginning to soften. Remove the skins and slice the shallots and peppers. Quarter the tomatoes.

2. Mix the fish sauce, lime juice and sugar and stir into the vegetables. Arrange on a bed of lettuce leaves and serve.

Serves 4

5 Cucumber Salad

Ingredients

1 cucumber, peeled and shredded
6 cherry tomatoes
2 spring onions, finely chopped
1 clove garlic, crushed
30 ml/2 tbsp lemon juice
30 ml/2 tbsp fish sauce
30 ml/2 tbsp caster sugar
2.5 ml/1/2 tsp chilli powder
1 fresh coriander sprig

Method

1. Mix together the cucumber, tomatoes, spring onions and garlic in a serving bowl.

2. Mix together the lemon juice, fish sauce, caster sugar and chilli powder and stir until the sugar has dissolved. Pour over the cucumber and mix well.

3. Garnish with the coriander and chill before serving.

Serves 4

Sweet and Sour Cucumber

Ingredients

1 large cucumber, peeled and thinly sliced
1 red onion, thinly sliced
1 dried red chilli pepper, chopped
45 ml/3 tbsp soft brown sugar
150 ml/ 1/4 pt/ 2/3 cup water
60 ml/4 tbsp white wine vinegar
Salt

Method

1. Place the cucumber, onion and chilli pepper in a bowl.

2. Dissolve the sugar in the water and vinegar, stirring continuously. Season with salt. Pour the mixture over the cucumber, stir well and chill until ready to serve.

Serves 4

7 Mango Salad

Ingredients

3 mangoes, sliced
5 ml/1 tsp salt
Juice of 2 limes
15 ml/1 tbsp groundnut oil
4 cloves garlic, crushed
5 spring onions, sliced
225 g/8 oz pork, minced
60 ml/4 tbsp fish sauce
60 ml/4 tbsp crunchy peanut butter
30 ml/2 tbsp soft brown sugar
Freshly ground black pepper

Method

1. Place the mango slices in a bowl and sprinkle with salt and lime juice.

2. Heat the oil and fry the garlic and spring onions for about 4 minutes until just soft. Remove from the pan and leave to drain.

3. Add the pork to the pan and fry until browned on all sides. Stir in the fish sauce, peanut butter and sugar and season with pepper. Remove from the heat and stir in the onions and garlic and the mango slices and lime juice. Mix thoroughly and chill until ready to serve.

Serves 4-6

8 Prawn and Orange Salad

Ingredients

225 g/8 oz cooked prawns
4 oranges, peeled and thinly sliced
1 dried red chilli pepper, crushed
2 cloves garlic, crushed
6 mint leaves, chopped
Salt
Juice of 1 lime
10 ml/2 tsp fish sauce

Method

1. Mix together the prawns and orange slices. Stir in the chilli pepper, garlic and mint, sprinkle with salt and mix the ingredients together well.

2. Mix together the lime juice and fish sauce. Pour over the salad and toss well. Chill before serving.

Serves 4

9 Sardine Salad

Ingredients

400 g/14 oz canned sardines in tomato sauce
60 ml/4 tbsp lime juice
1 stalk lemon grass, sliced
2 shallots, sliced
4 spring onions, chopped
1 red pepper, thinly sliced
30 ml/2 tbsp fish sauce
30 ml/2 tbsp chopped fresh mint
15 ml/1 tbsp chopped fresh basil
1 red lettuce

Method

1. Heat the sardines in their sauce for about 10 minutes. Cut them into chunks and mix with all the other ingredients except the lettuce. Mix together well.

2. Arrange the lettuce leaves on a serving plate and spoon the sardine mixture on top. Serve at once.

Serves 4

10 Spinach and Chicken Salad

Ingredients

225 g/8 oz spinach, shredded
45 ml/3 tbsp caster sugar
45 ml/3 tbsp lemon juice
30 ml/2 tbsp fish sauce
Pinch of cayenne pepper
225 g/8 oz cooked chicken, shredded
50 g/2 oz/^{1}/$_2$ cup roasted peanuts, chopped
2 carrots, grated

Method

1. Arrange the spinach on a serving plate.

2. Mix together the sugar, lemon juice, fish sauce and cayenne pepper and stir until the sugar has dissolved. Pour over the chicken and mix well.

3. Arrange the chicken on top of the spinach and sprinkle with the peanuts and carrots.

Serves 4

11 Water Chestnut Salad

Ingredients

15 ml/1 tbsp groundnut oil
2 spring onions, chopped
3 cloves garlic, chopped
1 dried red chilli pepper, chopped
30 ml/2 tbsp fish sauce
Juice of 2 limes
15 ml/1 tbsp sugar
225 g/8 oz canned water chestnuts, drained and cut into strips
100 g/4 oz cooked pork, chopped
100 g/4 oz cooked prawns, chopped
1 sprig coriander, chopped

Method

1. Heat the oil and fry the onions, garlic and chilli pepper for about 6 minutes until lightly browned. Remove from the heat and mix in the fish sauce, lime juice and sugar, stirring well.

2. Place the chestnuts in a serving bowl with the pork and prawns. Pour over the dressing and toss thoroughly. Serve sprinkle with coriander.

Serves 4

12 Watercress Salad

Ingredients

30 ml/2 tbsp corn oil
2 shallots, finely chopped
1 clove garlic, crushed
1 bunch watercress, chopped
10 cooked peeled prawns
2 slices cooked pork, diced
45 ml/3 tbsp roasted peanuts, chopped
30 ml/2 tbsp fish sauce
30 ml/2 tbsp lime juice
15 ml/1 tbsp granulated sugar
2 red chilli peppers, cut into strips

Method

1. Heat the oil and fry the shallots and garlic for about 4 minutes until soft. Remove from the pan and drain on kitchen paper.

2. Gently mix together the watercress, prawns, pork and peanuts.

3. Just before serving, mix together the fish sauce, lime juice and sugar, pour over the salad and toss gently. Sprinkle with the shallots and garlic and garnish with the chilli peppers.

Serves 4

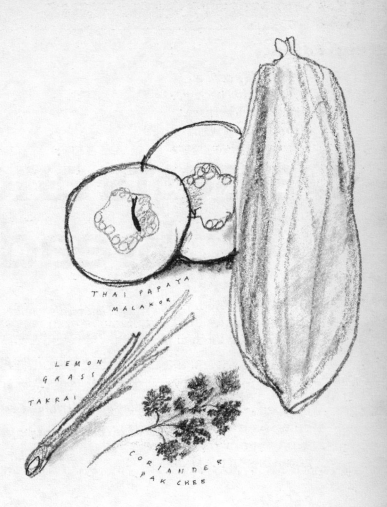

THAI PAPAYA
MALAKOR

LEMON
GRASS
TAKRAI

CORIANDER
PAK CHEE

Desserts and
Breads

*Most Thai meals would finish
with fresh fruits – whatever
varieties are available and in
season. However, for special
occasions, wonderful desserts are
served to complement perfectly a
spectacular meal.*

1 Banana Chips

Ingredients

4 small firm bananas
250 ml/8 fl oz/1 cup lime or lemon juice
Oil for deep-frying
225 g/8 oz/1 cup caster sugar

Method

1. Slice the bananas lengthways into thin strips and place them in a bowl. Pour over the lime or lemon juice and leave to stand for 10 minutes.

2. Heat the oil. Drain the banana slices thoroughly and deep-fry, in batches if necessary, for a few minutes until golden brown and crisp. Drain well on kitchen paper.

3. Coat the bananas in sugar and serve hot or cold.

Serves 4

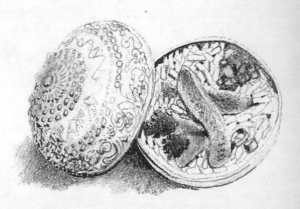

2 Fried Bananas

Ingredients

4 firm bananas
30 ml/2 tbsp butter or margarine
60 ml/4 tbsp soft brown sugar
Juice of 2 limes

Method

1. Slice the bananas in half lengthways then cut across into quarters. Heat the butter or margarine and fry the bananas for a few minutes until soft and golden brown.

2. Add the sugar and stir gently until the sugar dissolves and forms a syrup. Transfer to a warmed serving dish, sprinkle with lime juice and serve at once.

    Serves 4

3 Bananas with Coconut Milk

Ingredients

4 small bananas, cut into chunks
600 ml/1 pt/2 1/2 cups coconut milk
50 g/2 oz/ 1/4 cup soft brown sugar
Pinch of salt

Method

1. Steam the bananas over boiling water for about 20 minutes.

2. Bring the coconut milk, sugar and salt to the boil. Add the bananas, cover and simmer for 45 minutes. Serve hot.

Serves 4

Rainbow Coconut Pancakes

Ingredients

900 ml/1 1/2 pts/3 3/4 cups coconut milk
175 g/6 oz/1 1/2 cups rice flour
3 eggs, beaten
100 g/4 oz/ 1/2 cup granulated sugar
A pinch of salt
100 g/4 oz coconut flakes
Red and green food colouring
15 ml/1 tbsp vegetable oil

Method

1.   Beat the coconut milk, rice flour, eggs, sugar and
     salt to a smooth batter. Reserve a little of the
     coconut for decoration and stir the remainder into
     the batter. Divide between 3 bowls and colour one
     green and one red with a few drops of food
     colouring.

2.   Heat a very little oil in a pancake pan, pour in just
     enough batter to cover the surface and fry until the
     underside is cooked and spotted brown. Turn and
     cook the other side. Roll up the pancake and
     arrange on a warmed serving dish. Cook the
     remaining pancakes in the same way, keeping the
     others warm.

3.   Sprinkle the pancakes with the remaining coconut
     and serve at once.

Serves 4

5 Coconut Custard

Ingredients

100 g/4 oz/ 1/2 cup soft brown sugar
A pinch of salt
450 ml/ 3/4 pt/2 cups coconut milk
3 eggs, beaten

Method

1. Mix together the sugar, salt and coconut milk in a saucepan. Bring to the boil then reduce the heat and simmer gently for 25 minutes, stirring continuously, until reduced to about 250 ml/8 fl oz/1 cup. Leave to cool slightly.

2. Gradually whisk in the eggs.

3. Pour the mixture into a 20 cm/8 in square baking tin, stand in a steamer and steam over a saucepan of hot water for about 1 hour until a knife inserted into the centre comes out clean. Leave to cool and serve with sweet rice.

Serves 4

6 Lychees with Custard

Ingredients

5 eggs, separated
50 g/2 oz granulated sugar
450 ml/ ³/₄ pt/3 cups evaporated milk
16 lychees, peeled and stoned

Method

1. Whisk the egg whites until stiff. Place in a steamer basket and steam over a pan of hot water until just firm. Remove from the heat and set aside.

2. Beat the egg yolks and sugar over a low heat until pale then stir in the sugar and evaporated milk. Stir over a low heat until the mixture thickens to a smooth custard. Remove from the heat.

3. Place the lychees in a serving bowl and pour over the custard. Spoon the egg whites over the custard and chill until ready to serve.

4. As a variation, you can use melon balls instead of lychees.

Serves 4

7 Mangoes with Rice

Ingredients

> 3 mangoes
> 450 g/1 lb/2 cups cooked short-grain rice
> 250 ml/8 fl oz/1 cup coconut milk
> 45 ml/3 tbsp soft brown sugar
> Pinch of salt

Method

1. Wash the mangoes then chill them in the refrigerator.

2. Place the rice and coconut milk in a saucepan, bring to the boil and simmer for about 5 minutes until thick. Stir in the sugar and salt. Cover and simmer gently for about 4 minutes.

3. Meanwhile, peel and slice the mangoes thinly and arrange around the edge of a serving plate.

4. Turn out the rice or press it into a mould then arrange it in the centre of the mangoes.

Serves 4

8 Sweet Coconut Rice

Ingredients

450 g/1 lb/2 cups Thai sweet rice
1.2 l/2 pts/5 cups coconut milk
100 g/4 oz/¹/2 cup sugar
5 ml/1 tsp salt

Method

1. Wash the rice well and soak it for at least 2 hours. Drain well.

2. Place the rice in a bamboo steamer and steam over a pan of boiling water for about 15 minutes. Stir well then continue to steam for about 10 minutes until the rice is tender.

3. Meanwhile, mix together the coconut milk, sugar and salt in a heavy-based saucepan, bring to the boil then reduce the heat and simmer for about 20 minutes, stirring continuously, until about 250 ml/8 fl oz/1 cup remains.

4. Stir the cooked rice into the coconut milk, cover and leave to stand for 15 minutes. Serve warm.

Serves 4

9 | Sweet Black Beans

Ingredients

225 g/8 oz dried black beans
350 g/12 oz soft brown sugar
600 ml/1 pt/2 1/2 cups coconut milk
120 ml/4 fl oz/ 1/2 cup water
A pinch of salt

Method

1. Soak the black beans overnight in cold water.
    Drain and rinse thoroughly.

2. Place the beans in a saucepan and cover with fresh
    water. Bring to the boil and simmer for 1 hour until
    well done. Drain.

3. Mix together the sugar, coconut milk, water and
    salt in a saucepan. Bring to the boil, stirring until
    the sugar has dissolved. Add the beans and return
    to the boil. Remove from the heat and leave to cool
    slightly. Serve with rice or sliced mango.

Serves 4

10 | Mango Bread

Ingredients

175 g/6 oz/1 ½ cups plain flour
5 ml/1 tsp bicarbonate of soda
10 ml/2 tsp baking powder
Pinch of salt
25 g/1 oz/ ¼ cup desiccated coconut
30 ml/2 tbsp chopped mixed nuts
2 mangoes, chopped
50 g/2 oz/ ¼ cup butter or margarine, melted
15 ml/1 tbsp black treacle
Few drops of vanilla essence
2 eggs, beaten

Method

1. Mix together the flour, bicarbonate of soda, baking powder and salt.

2. Stir in the coconut and nuts. Stir in the mangoes, butter or margarine, treacle and vanilla essence. Gradually add enough egg to make a fairly soft mixture and stir until the mixture is well combined.

3. Pour into a greased and lined 900 g/2 lb loaf tin and bake in a preheated oven at 180°C/350°F/gas mark 4 for about 1 hour until well risen and golden brown.

Makes 1 x 900 g/2 lb loaf

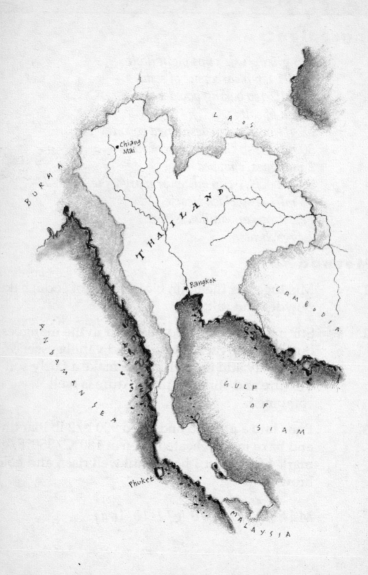

Drinks

Iced tea and coffee are popular in Thailand, and they differ from European drinks mainly in that they use tinned evaporated or condensed milk. Rice wine is also often served.

1 | Iced Coffee

Ingredients

> 150 ml/ ¼ pt/ ⅔ cup strong black coffee
> 250 ml/8 fl oz/1 cup boiling water
> 30 ml/2 tbsp sweetened condensed milk
> Ice cubes
> Mint sprigs to garnish

Method

1. Stir together the coffee, boiling water and condensed milk.

2. Place the ice cubes in tall glasses and pour the mixture into the glasses. Serve garnished with mint leaves.

3. You can make iced tea in the same way using strong tea instead of coffee.

Serves 4

2 Mango Crush

Ingredients

2 ripe mangoes, peeled and seeded
60 ml/4 tbsp rum
30 ml/2 tbsp lime juice
15 ml/1 tbsp soft brown sugar
Crushed ice

Method

1. Blend the mango, rum, lime juice and sugar in a food processor or blender. Gradually add the ice until the mixture is soft and slushy. Serve at once.

Serves 4

3 Limeade

Ingredients

6 limes
100 g/4 oz granulated sugar
750 ml/1 1/4 pts/3 cups boiling water
2.5 ml/ 1/2 tsp salt
Ice cubes

Method

1. Squeeze the lime juice into a jug, straining out the seeds.

2. Place the rinds in a second jug, cover with the sugar and pour over the boiling water. Leave to stand for 20 minutes. Stir in the salt.

3. Strain the liquid from the lime rinds into the juice, add the ice cubes and chill before serving.

Serves 4

Sauces

The Thais love a variety of sauces, especially curry and chilli sauces which vary from fairly mild to exceptionally hot. We have included a selection here to introduce you to the flavour sensations of Thai sauces.

1 Hot Chilli Sauce

Ingredients

200 g/7 oz canned tomatoes
225 g/8 oz sultanas
60 ml/4 tbsp white wine vinegar
1 dried red chilli pepper, chopped
2 fresh red chilli peppers, chopped
5 cloves garlic, crushed
5 ml/1 tsp salt
225 g/8 oz red plum jam
250 ml/8 fl oz/1 cup pineapple juice
60 ml/4 tbsp soft brown sugar

Method

1. Mix together the tomatoes, sultanas, wine vinegar, chilli peppers, garlic and salt and blend to a smooth paste in a food processor or blender.

2. Warm the jam, pineapple juice and sugar over a low heat, stirring until the sugar dissolves. Add the blended ingredients and bring to the boil, stirring. Simmer gently for about 20 minutes until thick. Store in airtight jars in the refrigerator.

Serves 4

2 Chilli and Nut Sauce

Ingredients

50 g/2 oz/¼ cup sugar
120 ml/4 fl oz/½ cup boiling water
120 ml/4 fl oz/½ cup red wine vinegar
15 ml/1 tbsp fish sauce
1 red chilli pepper, finely chopped
1 small carrot, grated
30 ml/2 tbsp peanuts, chopped

Method

1. Dissolve the sugar in the boiling water, stirring well.

2. Mix in the wine vinegar, fish sauce and chilli pepper. Sprinkle with the carrot.

3. Leave to cool then chill thoroughly. Sprinkle with peanuts before serving with grilled meats or vegetables.

Serves 4

3 Crab Sauce

Ingredients

100 g/4 oz crab meat, flaked
450 ml/ ¾ pt/2 cups coconut cream
2.5 ml/½ tsp salt
1 onion, finely chopped
5 ml/1 tsp granulated sugar
2.5 ml/½ tsp tamarind paste
1 green chilli pepper, chopped
15 ml/1 tbsp chopped fresh coriander

Method

1.   Mix together the crab meat, coconut cream and salt in a heavy-based saucepan and bring slowly to the boil, stirring continuously. Reduce the heat and simmer for 5 minutes, stirring occasionally.

2.   Add the onion and sugar. Dissolve the tamarind paste in a little hot water and stir it into the pan with the chilli peppers. Simmer for a further 5 minutes, stirring occasionally. Transfer to a serving bowl and sprinkle with coriander. Serve with fried fish or steamed rice dishes.

Serves 4

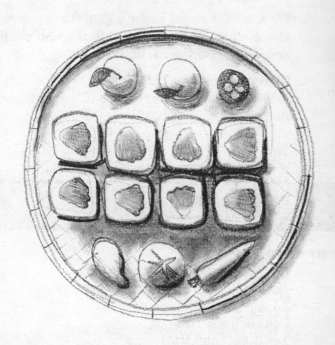

4 Cucumber Sauce

Ingredients

1 small cucumber, peeled and thinly sliced
50 g/2 oz/¼ cup sugar
250 ml/8 fl oz/1 cup boiling water
120 ml/4 fl oz/½ cup wine vinegar
5 ml/1 tsp salt
2 shallots, finely chopped
2 red chilli peppers, finely chopped

Method

1. Arrange the cucumber slices in a bowl.

2. Dissolve the sugar in the water, stirring well. Mix in the wine vinegar, salt, shallots and chilli peppers and pour over the cucumber.

3. Cover and chill until required.

Serves 4

5 Lime Sauce

Ingredients

60 ml/4 tbsp fish sauce
60 ml/4 tbsp lime juice
1 clove garlic, chopped
3 chilli peppers, chopped
5 ml/1 tsp sugar

Method

1.   Mix together all the ingredients, stirring until the sugar has dissolved.

2.   Serve with fried dishes and seafood.

Serves 4

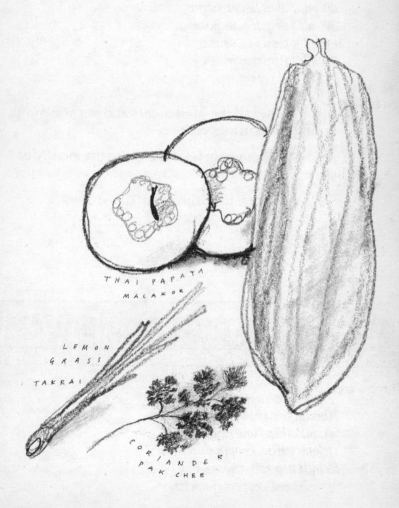

THAI PAPAYA
MALAKOR

LEMON
GRASS

TAKRAI

CORIANDER
PAK CHEE

6 Spiced Fish Sauce

Ingredients

1 dried red pepper, chopped
2 cloves garlic, crushed
60 ml/4 tbsp caster sugar
30 ml/2 tbsp lemon juice
60 ml/4 tbsp fish sauce
30 ml/2 tbsp water

Method

1.   Mix together all the ingredients and stir well until the sugar has dissolved.

2.   Add a little more water if the sauce is too salty or strong.

3.   Serve in a bowl to sprinkle on Thai dishes.

Serves 4

7 Sweet and Sour Sauce

Ingredients

225 g/8 oz sugar
150 ml/ 1/4 pt/ 2/3 cup water
60 ml/4 tbsp wine vinegar
15 ml/1 tbsp tomato purée
5 ml/1 tsp salt
1 dried red pepper, chopped

Method

1.   Place all the ingredients in a saucepan and heat gently, stirring until the sugar dissolves.

2.   Check and adjust the seasoning to taste.

Serves 4

8 Peanut Sauce

Ingredients

60 ml/4 tbsp vegetable oil
1 onion, finely chopped
1 clove garlic, chopped
1 red chilli pepper, chopped
5 ml/1 tsp grated lemon rind
2.5 ml/ 1/2 tsp curry powder
300 ml/ 1/2 pt/1 1/4 cups coconut milk
100 g/4 oz crunchy peanut butter
2 bay leaves
45 ml/3 tbsp soft brown sugar
45 ml/3 tbsp lemon juice
15 ml/1 tbsp fish sauce
5 ml/1 tsp tamarind paste
5 ml/1 tsp ground cinnamon

Method

1. Heat the oil and fry the onion, garlic, chilli pepper, lemon rind and curry powder for about 4 minutes until the onions are soft.

2. Add the remaining ingredients and stir well until they are thoroughly mixed. Simmer over a gentle heat for about 40 minutes until the sauce thickens, stirring frequently to make sure the mixture does not stick to the base of the pan. Adjust the seasoning to taste.

Serves 4

9 | Curry Paste

Ingredients

15 *red chilli peppers, soaked and chopped*
1 *stick lemon grass, chopped*
2 *shallots, sliced*
2 *cloves garlic, chopped*
30 *ml/2 tbsp vegetable oil*
15 *ml/1 tbsp chopped ginger root*
15 *ml/1 tbsp coriander seeds*
5 *ml/1 tsp grated lime rind*
5 *ml/1 tsp cumin seeds*
5 *ml/1 tsp salt*
5 *ml/1 tsp soft brown sugar*
5 *ml/1 tsp fish sauce*
2.5 *ml/ 1/2 tsp ground cinnamon*

Method

1. Blend all the ingredients together in a blender or food processor until smooth. Store in a screw-top jar in the refrigerator.

2. Use to make traditional Thai curries. Increase the number of chilli peppers used to make the paste hotter.

Makes 150 ml/ 1/4 pt/ 2/3 cup

10 | Yellow Curry Paste

Ingredients

5 yellow chilli peppers, chopped
1 stick lemon grass, chopped
2 shallots, sliced
2 cloves garlic, chopped
30 ml/2 tbsp vegetable oil
15 ml/1 tbsp soft brown sugar
5 ml/1 tsp chopped ginger root
5 ml/1 tsp curry powder
5 ml/1 tsp mustard powder
5 ml/1 tsp salt
5 ml/1 tsp coriander seeds
5 ml/1 tsp caraway seeds
2.5 ml/1/2 tsp ground cinnamon

Method

1. Blend all the ingredients together in a blender or food processor until smooth. Store in a screw-top jar in the refrigerator.

2. Use to make mild curries.

Makes 150 ml/ 1/4 pt / 2/3 cup

11 Red Curry Paste

Ingredients

15 red chilli peppers, chopped
2 sticks lemon grass, chopped
4 shallots, chopped
2 cloves garlic, chopped
30 ml/2 tbsp vegetable oil
15 ml/1 tbsp chopped ginger root
15 ml/1 tbsp fish sauce
5 ml/1 tsp grated lime rind
2.5 ml/$^{1}/_{2}$ tsp ground coriander
2.5 ml/$^{1}/_{2}$ tsp caraway seeds

Method

1. Combine all the ingredients in a food processor or blender and blend to a smooth paste. Store in a screw-top jar in the refrigerator.

Makes 150 ml/ $^{1}/_{4}$ pt/ $^{2}/_{3}$ cup

12 Green Curry Paste

Ingredients

15 green chilli peppers, chopped
3 sticks lemon grass, chopped
4 shallots, chopped
2 cloves garlic, chopped
30 ml/2 tbsp vegetable oil
15 ml/1 tbsp chopped ginger root
15 ml/1 tbsp fish sauce
15 ml/1 tbsp sugar
5 ml/1 tsp shrimp paste
5 ml/1 tsp grated lime rind
2.5 ml/1/2 tsp ground coriander
2.5 ml/1/2 tsp caraway seeds

Method

1. Combine all the ingredients in a food processor or blender and blend to a smooth paste. Store in a screw-top jar in the refrigerator.

   Makes 150 ml/ 1/4 pt / 2/3 cup

Index

Appetisers
Beef Satay 29
Coconut Squid Kebabs 20-21
Crispy Tofu 25
Crispy-Fried Noodles 19
Deep-Fried Fish Cakes 18
Fried Chicken Drumsticks 26
Grilled Scallops 22
Kebabs with Peanut Sauce 27
Sweet and Sour Eggs 24
Thai Meatballs 28
Asparagus, Prawns with 52

Bamboo Shoots 8
Chicken with Bamboo Shoots 66
Bananas
Banana Chips 125
Bananas with Coconut Milk 127
Fried Bananas 126
Basil
Prawn and Basil Stir-Fry 51
Prawns and Squid with Basil 53
Scallops with Basil 55
Bass with Ginger Sauce 42-3
Bean Sauce 8
Beans
Ginger Beans 90
Sweet Black Beans 134
Beansprouts, Fried 93
Beef
Beef Fried Rice 106
Beef Salad 110
Beef Satay 29
Beef with Noodles 76
Beef with Oyster Sauce 77
Thai Beef Curry 75
Thai Egg Rolls 84-5
Black Beans, Sweet 134
Bread, Mango 135
Broccoli
Broccoli Stir-Fry 92
Rice Noodles with Broccoli 102

Cabbage Salad 111
Cashew Nuts, Chicken with 65
Chicken
Chicken and Rice Soup 32
Chicken Fried Rice 107
Chicken with Bamboo Shoots 66

Chicken with Cashew Nuts 65
Chicken with Water Chestnuts 64
Fried Chicken Drumsticks 26
Ginger Chicken Soup 33
Grilled Chicken 63
Lemon Chicken and
Vegetable Soup 34
Minted Chicken Salad 112
Panaeng Chicken Curry 62
Rice Noodles with Chicken 100
Spinach and Chicken Salad 120
Stuffed Omelette 69
Sweet and Sour Chicken 68
Thai Chicken Curry 60-61
Chilli Peppers 8
Chilli and Nut Sauce 144
Chilli Fried Rice 105
Chilli Pepper Salad 113
Hot Chilli Pork 78
Hot Chilli Prawns 54
Hot Chilli Sauce 143
Mussels with Chilli Peppers 57
preparing 14
Clams with Ginger 56
Coconut Cream 8
Coconut Squid Kebabs 20-21
Coconut Milk 8
Bananas with Coconut Milk 127
Coconut Custard 130
Rainbow Coconut Pancakes 128
Sweet Coconut Rice 133
Coffee, Iced 138
cooking methods 14
Courgettes, Stuffed 94
Crab Sauce 144-5
Cucumber
Cucumber Salad 114
Cucumber Sauce 146
Sweet and Sour Cucumber 116
Curry
Fish Curry 48
Green Pork Curry 80
Panaeng Chicken Curry 62
Sweet Seafood Curry 50
Thai Beef Curry 75
Thai Chicken Curry 60-61
Curry Paste 151
Green Curry Paste 154
Red Curry Paste 153
Yellow Curry Paste 152

Custard
Coconut Custard 130
Lychees with Custard 131

Desserts
Banana Chips 125
Bananas with Coconut Milk 127
Coconut Custard 130
Fried Bananas 126
Lychees with Custard 131
Mangoes with Rice 132
Rainbow Coconut Pancakes 128
Sweet Black Beans 134
Sweet Coconut Rice 133
Drinks
Iced Coffee 138
Limeade 140
Mango Crush 139
Duck
Duck with Ginger and Garlic 71
Roast Duck 72

Eggs
Egg Noodles with Thick Sauce 97
Pork Omelette 83
Stuffed Omelette 69
Sweet and Sour Eggs 24
Thai Egg Rolls 84-5
equipment 13

Fish
Baked Fish Parcels 44
Bass with Ginger Sauce 42-3
Deep-Fried Fish Cakes 18
Fish Curry 48
fish sauce 9
Fish Soup 38
Mackerel with Garlic 45
Sole in Tamarind Sauce 47
Spiced Fish Sauce 148
Thai Fried Herring 46

Garlic
Duck with Ginger and Garlic 71
Mackerel with Garlic 45
Ginger 9
Bass with Ginger Sauce 42-3
Clams with Ginger 56
Duck with Ginger and Garlic 71
Ginger Beans 90
Ginger Chicken Soup 33

Herbs 9
Herring, Thai Fried 46

ingredients 8-11

Kebabs
Coconut Squid Kebabs 20-21
Kebabs with Peanut Sauce 27

Lemon Chicken and
Vegetable Soup 34
Lemon Grass 9
Limes 9
Lime Sauce 146-7
Limeade 140
Lychees with Custard 131

Mackerel with Garlic 45
Mangoes
Mango Bread 135
Mango Crush 139
Mango Salad 117
Mangoes with Rice 132
Meat
Beef Fried Rice 106
Beef Salad 110
Beef Satay 29
Beef with Noodles 76
Beef with Oyster Sauce 77
Green Pork Curry 80
Hot Chilli Pork 78
Minced Pork and Prawns 82
Pork Omelette 83
Pork Satay with Peanut Sauce 79
Quick Stir-Fried Pork 81
Thai Beef Curry 75
Thai Egg Rolls 84-5
Meatballs, Thai 28
Minted Chicken Salad 112
mortar and pestle 13
Mushrooms
dried mushrooms 9-10
Prawn and Mushroom Soup 39
Mussels with Chilli Peppers 57

Noodles 10
Beef with Noodles 76
Crispy-Fried Noodles 19
Egg Noodles with Thick Sauce 97
Mixed Vegetables Noodles 98
Rice Noodles 99
Rice Noodles with Broccoli 102
Rice Noodles with Chicken 100
Nuts
Chicken with Cashew Nuts 65
Chilli and Nut Sauce 144

Omelettes
Pork Omelette 83
Stuffed Omelette 69

Oranges
  Prawn and Orange Salad 118
Oyster Sauce 10, 77

Pancakes, Rainbow Coconut 128
Peanuts
  Chilli and Nut Sauce 144
  Kebabs with Peanut Sauce 27
  Peanut Sauce 150
  Pork Satay with Peanut Sauce 79
  Vegetables with Peanut Sauce 89
pestle and mortar 13
Pork
  Green Pork Curry 80
  Hot Chilli Pork 78
  Minced Pork and Prawns 82
  Pork Omelette 83
  Pork Satay with Peanut Sauce 79
  Quick Stir-Fried Pork 81
  Thai Egg Rolls 84-5
pots, clay 13
Poultry
  Chicken and Rice Soup 32
  Chicken Fried Rice 107
  Chicken with Bamboo Shoots 66
  Chicken with Cashew Nuts 65
  Chicken with Water Chestnuts 64
  Duck with Ginger and Garlic 71
  Fried Chicken Drumsticks 26
  Ginger Chicken Soup 33
  Grilled Chicken 63
  Grilled Quail 70
  Lemon Chicken and
    Vegetable Soup 34
  Minted Chicken Salad 112
  Panaeng Chicken Curry 62
  Rice Noodles with Chicken 100
  Roast Duck 72
  Spinach and Chicken Salad 120
  Stuffed Omelette 69
  Sweet and Sour Chicken 68
  Thai Chicken Curry 60-61
Prawns 10
  Corn and Prawn Soup 37
  Hot and Sour Prawn and
    Vegetable Soup 36
  Hot Chilli Prawns 54
  Minced Pork and Prawns 82
  Prawn and Basil Stir-Fry 51
  Prawn and Mushroom Soup 39
  Prawn and Orange Salad 118
  Prawns and Squid with Basil 53
  Prawns with Asparagus 52

Quail, Grilled 70

Rice 10
  Beef Fried Rice 106
  Chicken and Rice Soup 32
  Chicken Fried Rice 107
  Chilli Fried Rice 105
  Mangoes with Rice 132
  Red Fried Rice 104
  Rice Noodles 99
  Rice Noodles with Broccoli 102
  Rice Noodles with Chicken 100
  Sweet Coconut Rice 133
  Thai Rice 103

Salads ....
  Beef Salad 110
  Cabbage Salad 111
  Chilli Pepper Salad 113
  Cucumber Salad 114
  Mango Salad 117
  Minted Chicken Salad 112
  Prawn and Orange Salad 118
  Sardine Salad 119
  Spinach and Chicken Salad 120
  Sweet and Sour Cucumber 116
  Water Chestnut Salad 121
  Watercress Salad 122
Sardine Salad 119
Satay
  Beef Satay 29
  Pork Satay with Peanut Sauce 79
Sauces
  Chilli and Nut Sauce 144
  Crab Sauce 144-5
  Cucumber Sauce 146
  Curry Paste 151
  fish sauce 9
  Ginger Sauce 42-3
  Green Curry Paste 154
  Hot Chilli Sauce 143
  Lime Sauce 146-7
  Oyster Sauce, 10 77
  Peanut Sauce 27, 79, 89, 150
  Red Curry Paste 153
  Spiced Fish Sauce 148
  Sweet and Sour Sauce 148-9
  Tamarind Sauce 47
  Thick Sauce 97
  Yellow Curry Paste 152
Scallops
  Grilled Scallops 22
  Scallops with Basil 55
Seafood
  Sweet Seafood Curry 50
  see also Clams; Mussels; Prawns;
  Scallops
Shallots 10

Shellfish 10
Shrimp Paste 11
Sole in Tamarind Sauce 47
Soups
   Chicken and Rice Soup 32
   Corn and Prawn Soup 37
   Fish Soup 38
   Ginger Chicken Soup 33
   Hot and Sour Prawn and
   Vegetable Soup 34
   Lemon Chicken and
   Vegetable Soup 34
   Prawn and Mushroom Soup 39
Spices 9
Spinach and Chicken Salad 120
Squid
   Coconut Squid Kebabs 20-21
   Prawns and Squid with Basil 53
steamer 13
Sweetcorn
   Corn and Prawn Soup 37

Tamarind 11

Sole in Tamarind Sauce 47
Tofu, Crispy 25
tomatoes, skinning 14

Vegetables
   Hot and Sour Prawn and
   Vegetable Soup 36
   Lemon Chicken and
   Vegetable Soup 34
   Mixed Vegetables Noodles 98
   Sweet and Sour Stir-Fry 88
   Vegetables with Peanut Sauce 89
   see also under individual vegetables

Water Chestnuts
   Chicken with Water Chestnuts 64
   Water Chestnut Salad 121
Watercress Salad 122
wok 13
Won Ton Wrappers 11

Yellow Bean Paste 11